Spare Time Guides, No. 2

SPARE TIME GUIDES SERIES

Ann J. Harwell, Editor

No. 1 *Automotive Repair and Maintenance.* By Robert G. Schipf.

No. 2 *Hunting and Fishing.* By Cecil F. Clotfelter.

No. 3 *Home Repair and Improvement.* By Robert G. Schipf.

No. 4 *Crafts for Today: Ceramics, Glasscrafting, Leatherworking, Candlemaking, and Other Popular Crafts.* By Rolly M. Harwell and Ann J. Harwell.

No. 5 *Stamps and Coins.* By Richard H. Rosichan.

SPARE TIME GUIDES:
Information Sources for Hobbies and Recreation, No. 2

Hunting and Fishing

CECIL F. CLOTFELTER

1974
Libraries Unlimited, Inc.
Littleton, Colorado

Library of Congress Card Number 73-90569
International Standard Book Number 0-87287-079-0

LIBRARIES UNLIMITED, INC.
P.O. Box 263
Littleton, Colorado 80120

CONTENTS

PREFACE

The Spare Time Guides series was conceived with a dual purpose—to provide libraries with selective annotated lists of recommended books on specific hobbies and recreational activities, and to help craftsmen and do-it-yourselfers learn more about their hobbies and crafts.

The current upsurge of interest in hobbies and crafts for young and old alike has brought with it a proliferation of books for these readers. Beginning as well as advanced craftsmen find it difficult to choose useful books that fit their skills and interests. At present, few selection aids on crafts are available. The reviewing media that serve librarians devote little space to books on crafts and leisure time activities. A search of hobby and craft magazines reveals only a few book reviews. In too many cases librarians and hobbyists alike are left to rely on the exaggerated claims of advertisers or other equally unsatisfactory channels for information about these important books. The Spare Time Guides series is designed to fill this gap.

The guides are similar in format, with slight variations depending on the requirements of a particular subject. Each guide lists the most important works for a given topic—generally works that are in print and readily available—providing complete bibliographic description and annotations that are both descriptive and critical. Periodicals are listed in a separate section. Appended material includes a list of national or important regional organizations, a directory of major publishers in the field, a directory of suppliers and manufacturers (where appropriate), and an author-title-subject index.

The present volume, No. 2 in the series, fills a long-standing need for a bibliography of works on hunting, fishing, and related activities. Its 168 entries for books are divided primarily into chapters on hunting, fishing, firearms, and archery, with a preliminary chapter on general encyclopedias, dictionaries, and guides. Bibliographical descriptions give author, title, publisher, place and date of publication, pagination, price, LC number, and International Standard Book Number. The long annotations (about 100 to 200 words) are informative and critical and will provide substantial guidance to those seeking a book for a specific purpose.

Chapters 7 and 8 list periodicals (26 entries) and national organizations, giving full address and a short description of each. A directory of publishers and one of manufacturers and suppliers form the concluding chapters. The author, title, and subject index provides access to all entries by entry number.

Cecil F. Clotfelter, Technical Services Librarian at Eastern New Mexico University in Portales, is an experienced and enthusiastic hunter and fisherman. His introduction and his eminently readable annotations reflect his wide knowledge of the subjects at hand.

Any hunter, fisherman, firearms buff, or archer who has ever sought a specific title in publishers' catalogs, on bookstore shelves, or in the local branch library's card catalog will recognize the value of the *Hunting and Fishing* volume of the Spare Time Guides series. And any budget-conscious librarian who has been confronted with interminable lists of books on crafts, hobbies, and recreation—and who has despaired of choosing the right book for the right audience—will, we hope, find the volumes of the Spare Time Guides series to be helpful selection tools and reference sources.

Ann J. Harwell
Editor, Spare Time Guides

Dedicated to my father, C. F. Clotfelter, 1893-1964,
who passed on to me his love for hunting,
fishing, and the out-of-doors.

Chapter 1

INTRODUCTION

At the present time there are no available bibliographies, either comprehensive or selective, for the general fields of hunting, fishing, or firearms. This *selective bibliography* is offered in the hope that it will serve as a buying guide for libraries seeking to serve a wider clientele; as a selection guide for sportsmen since it is unlikely that any one bookstore will have available on their shelves all the books included herein, and as a guide to information sources for firearms collectors, museums, and dealers in arms, ammunition, hunting equipment, fishing tackle, and all accessories for the three major activities in this compilation.

Selection of books to be included was based on two primary points. First, with only a few exceptions, all books are currently in print and may be purchased at reasonable prices through normal book trade channels, and all periodicals may be received by subscription. The second point concerns the quality of the book. This is essentially subjective; few books exist that are totally error-free. Errors can be factual or simply the result of misleading wording; I don't believe that either form of error is intentional on the part of the authors. The subjective judgment of one reader with regard to quality may not coincide with the subjective judgment of another because of differing backgrounds, experiences, and opinions. This volume itself is not exempt from the above possible faults, but as a trained gunsmith, a life-long hunter and fisherman, and a practicing librarian, I have tried to look at each book from each applicable point of view.

A few books on hunting and fishing in other parts of the world have been listed, but for the most part the emphasis is on these sports in their most common forms in the United States and throughout the North American continent. Many localized activities were excluded either through lack of material or because of limited interest. Most of the works on firearms are historical, heavily illustrated, and of greatest value to the collector or dealer. Juvenile materials were omitted since there seem to be few items worthy of note on the current market, but teenagers will have no trouble reading or enjoying nearly everything here.

The main body of the bibliography is in classified arrangement. Within each division entries are subdivided by more specific topics where necessary, and works within each part are listed alphabetically by author. Periodicals and publishers are listed alphabetically, but the list of organizations and the selective directory of manufacturers, dealers, and suppliers are both arranged by subject. *Thomas Register of Manufacturers* may be consulted in most libraries for the names and addresses of other manufacturers.

A consideration of the American heritage and experience concerning hunting, fishing, and firearms leads to the conclusion that America is a land of hunters and fishermen. It is a relatively young nation in the family of nations of the world; the western hemisphere was discovered only four hundred and eighty-one years ago by Europeans, beginning the count with the voyage of Columbus; European and Asian civilizations were ancient before we got started. The early settlers of this nation lived off the land–hunting, fishing, gathering wild fruits, berries, roots, and herbs–until such advances had been made that they could grow or raise their own food. It has been less than one hundred years since the end of the frontier, and up to that point wild game was an essential addition to the livelihood of the settlers. The heritage of hunting and fishing in America is of more recent memory than that heritage in older nations.

In spite of attacks by some pressure groups attempting to ban hunting or fishing, the Bureau of Outdoor Recreation of the U.S. Department of the Interior reported that in 1965 (latest figures available) there were 32,881,000 persons in the United States who fished and/or hunted, and for all activities–food, lodging, travel, bait, equipment, etc.–they spent a total of $4,046,440,000. This is a nice piece of change in anyone's language. The recreational value of all this activity cannot be measured in terms of money, nor can the value of food derived from the fields and streams of the country. Hunters, fishermen, shooters, and archers do more to support conservation efforts with their money than do all other groups combined. They also donate vast amounts of time and labor. Years ago sportsmen asked that a tax be added to sports equipment and that the revenue be earmarked for conservation—to preserve wetlands for waterfowl and some of the fur-bearing animals, to buy and maintain wildlife refuges and game preserves—and for research in game and wildlife management to assure the continuance of our native birds, animals, and fish. There have been attempts by political leaders to remove the tax, but sportsmen have insisted that it be continued.

The collecting of guns as a hobby or for financial gain is so closely connected to the hunting interest that it cannot be omitted. Few persons outside the hunting/gun collecting fraternity realize the vast numbers of makes, models, and calibers of firearms that have been manufactured in this country since its beginning. A gunsmith for whom I worked at one time had been a gunsmith, trader, and dealer for over 40 years at that time, yet hardly a week passed that he did not encounter a firearm that he had never heard of before it came into his shop. The firearms books included herein will furnish much information both for the private collector and for the dealer who trades, buys, and sells guns for profit.

A slogan that one sees occasionally says, "God does not deduct from man's allotted span the time spent fishing." Recreation becomes more and more precious in the crowded society in which we all live; if the above slogan is true, a great many people are trying to extend their lives by spending time afield. Since the second best thing for those who enjoy hunting and fishing is reading about others who have like interests, this guide is presented in the hope that busy people will be able to choose more readily the books and periodicals that will best suit their needs.

I would like to acknowledge, with thanks, the help and encouragement of Libraries Unlimited in proposing a publication to help serve the needs of America's hunters, fishermen, archers, and gun enthusiasts; the support of my wife, Mary, through the time and effort she spent typing, proofreading, and nagging (in a nice way) whenever I put off work that needed to be done.

June 30, 1973 Cecil F. Clotfelter

Chapter 2

ENCYCLOPEDIAS, DICTIONARIES, GUIDES

Hunting

1. Jefferson, John, comp. **Hunters Guide to Texas**. Austin, Tex., Jenkins Publishing Co., 1971. 247p. illus. $3.95pa.

The largest of the 48 contiguous states, Texas covers a lot of land and a wide variety of climates and game habitats, inhabited by a great diversity of game animals and birds. The compiler states with Texas pride that one can hunt for mule deer, whitetail, turkey, quail, coyote, and crow, all in one month without leaving the state. His explanation of the hunting lease system should be very helpful to visitors and newcomers to Texas; it also explains why so many Texans do much of their hunting in New Mexico, Colorado, Arizona, and Wyoming where public lands are accessible. Jefferson divides the state into seven regions according to the general nature of habitat and hunting conditions; lease information is included for each region. Deer hunting receives the greatest amount of attention, although other game is discussed adequately. The Hill Country region has the greatest concentration of deer, and deer hunting is the number one sport of the region (talking about deer hunting is number two, and lying about deer hunting is number three). All other sports are further down the list of importance. Exotics—foreign imports—are available on several private game preserves for those who wish to pay the price and hunt mouflon, axis deer, blackbuck, and others. The guide, updated annually, is well done, but its appeal is largely limited to Texans trying to find a place to hunt.

2. Kozicky, Edward, John Madson, and David Petzal, comps. **Winchester Hunter's Handbook.** New York, Winchester, 1972. 191p. illus. $1.95. LC 72-79368. ISBN 0-87691-087-8pa.

The current issue of an annual series, the handbook surveys and forecasts hunting prospects for all types of game in all 50 states and the Canadian provinces and territories. Information on seasons, prospects, best hunting areas, and license fees, requirements, and restrictions have been provided by the fish and game departments of each state or province. As a bonus addition to the basic data, there are articles on the many aspects of hunting, firearms and accessories, manners in the field, ballistics and statistics. The total compilation is a concise collection of facts to help the hunter to better plan his trip for greater success and enjoyment.

3. **New Hunter's Encyclopedia.** 3rd ed. Ed. by James B. Trefethen and Leonard Miracle. Harrisburg, Pa., Stackpole, 1970. (Repr. of 1966 ed.) 1131p. illus. index. $24.95. LC 66-12713.

Divided into several major sections, the *New Hunter's Encyclopedia* covers more material pertinent to its subject than four or five volumes of more specialized works without sacrificing very much that is of interest to the probable user. The first seven sections deal with the life histories and hunting information of North American large and small game animals, game birds, and predators. Life histories are more extensive and more readable than those found in the various "Fieldbook . . ." series, although some of the more detailed technical points have been omitted. Life histories are adequate for the hunter, the wildlife watcher and amateur biologist, and perhaps even for most college students at the introductory level. A color section of game birds for identification purposes is beautifully done. Firearms information, in four parts, provides excellent coverage of hunting rifles, shotguns, and pistols and their ammunition, with photographs of representative makes and models currently available. Laws governing handguns in the 50 states, Canada, Mexico, Puerto Rico and the Virgin Islands are discussed in summary form, but the reader should be aware of the possibility, and probability, of changes in laws and of new laws governing rifles and shotguns since the passage of the 1968 Gun Control Act by Congress. Archery hunting, the preservation of meat and trophies, and the process of tanning game hides completes the information of interest to hunters only. Camping information, with recipes for the camp cook, clothing for hunters and campers, bedding and tents and other shelters are of use to all who enjoy the out-of-doors. The amateur shutterbug has not been forgotten in this excellent work, but for those who delve more deeply into photography a more comprehensive and technical publication will be of greater value, since the information here consists primarily of pointers for better hunting and wildlife shots. Federal laws pertaining to wildlife, hunting laws of the states, the Canadian provinces, and Mexico, an extensive glossary of terms and an excellent index complete the volume. Well-bound, well-printed, and well-illustrated, the *Encyclopedia* is a valuable addition to any library.

Fishing

4. Allyn, Rube. **A Dictionary of Fishes**. 11th ed. St. Petersburg, Fla., Great Outdoors Pub. Co., 1967. 128p. illus. index. $1.95. SBN 8200-0101-5pa.

Although "dictionary" is part of the title, arrangement is not in true dictionary format and the index must be used to locate individual species. Most of the approximately seven hundred fish described are pictured. Common names, Latin names, size, edibility (in most cases), colors, and habitat are given for each one in a brief statement. Salt and fresh water species are both included. Those that are dangerous to man, such as certain sharks, rays, scorpionfish, and others that are poisonous or electrified are identified. Eight pages of full-color illustrations, in addition to all the black and white ones, help relieve the impression of ugliness of some of the more atrocious varieties; but only another lionfish could really be attracted to a lionfish.

5. Bauer, Erwin A., ed. **Fishermen's Digest**. 8th ed. Northfield, Ill., Digest Books, 1971. 320p. illus. $5.95. LC 75-148727. ISBN 0-695-80217-8pa.

Here is a collection of 59 articles on all kinds of fishing by many well-known fishermen who write extensively about their sport. Salt water, fresh water streams, lakes, farm ponds; albacore, bass, trout, or carp—they are all here. There are also articles on tackle of all sorts, lures, camping equipment, and camp trailers or coaches recommended for the angler. Every page is packed with information and the reader has only to choose his target or define his need to find answers and advice. Each article is well illustrated with photos. A directory of manufacturers of fishing tackle is added.

6. Chaplin, Charles C. G. **Fishwatchers Guide to West Atlantic Coral Reefs**. Illus. by Peter Scott. Wynnewood, Pa., Livingston Pub. Co., 1972. 64p. illus. index. $5.95. LC 72-9309. ISBN 0-87098-047-5.

East coast skin divers, snorklers, and swimmers should be overjoyed with the publication of this guide in full color, printed on a waterproof, washable, grease-proof opaque plastic. It can be taken underwater to help in the identification of more than 160 species. Presumably the colors of the illustrations would be dulled by depth in approximately the same proportion as the colors of the fish. Common names, technical names, maximum sizes, and general information about each specie is given in brief, but no information is included about poisonous or dangerous fish that might be encountered. It would be helpful to have a hole punched in one corner for hanging the guide from a belt. Fishermen will have some use for this volume even though many of the fish identified are not commonly sought by the angler and others are rarely caught. In addition to the 23 color plates, each of which shows six to ten different fishes, there is a section of outline drawings of other species or varieties closely related to those shown in color.

7. Consumer Guide. **Consumer Guide Fishing Equipment Test Reports**. New York, Pocket Books, 1973. 386p. illus. glossary. $1.95.

With the enormous variety of products available in any given field, the consumer is hard pressed to determine the best qualities and values that he is receiving for his hard-earned money. There are a number of firms or agencies engaged in testing products and reporting the test results. Consumer Guide currently has in print evaluations on guns, cars, bicycles, photographic equipment and fishing equipment. This latter volume analyzes the needs in different types of fishing, the level of expertise of the fisherman, and advises on the equipment to be purchased. Their statement that the beginner should not invest heavily in expensive equipment because he might find that fishing was not his cup of tea is wise, but neither should the novice skimp to the point that he is discouraged and turned off by poor equipment. History of fishing, tackle, accessories, best buys in rods and reels, price listing, and the newer electronic fishing gear are all covered well. Heavily illustrated, the pictorial charts on hooks, sinkers, gaffs, nets, etc., are good for quick reference. The user of this guide should remember that prices may vary widely in different areas of the country and at different seasons of the year, and that manufacturers are constantly changing models and styles.

8. Konizeski, Dick. **The Montanans' Fishing Guide. Vol. II: Montana Waters East of Continental Divide.** Missoula, Mont., Mountain Press, 1970. 359p. illus. $3.95pa. LC 75-122314. SBN 87842-016-9.

The second of a two-volume set, this guide concerns itself with fishing waters east of the Continental Divide in Montana; more particularly, it deals with the less accessible waters in primitive or wilderness areas, although some easily reached streams and lakes are included. Organization is by drainage system in alphabetical order, then by tributaries and lakes within the system, also in alphabetical order. Directions are given for reaching each spot, and there is a description of the area as well as comments on the quality of fishing and the species to be caught. Seasonal changes in weather and rainfall may affect fishing in any water, so anyone traveling a long distance for angling should check with local experts. No maps are included, and the highway maps put out by service stations are not always adequate; local inquiry may again be necessary. Maps published and sold separately as companions to the guide are available in most magazine and book shops. The guide should be very useful; the author may have revealed some of the favorite "secret" fishing holes of the local citizens.

9. McClane, A. J. **The "Field and Stream" International Fishing Guide.** Special rev. pocket ed. New York, Scribner's, 1973. 224p. maps. $3.95pa. LC 72-12166. SBN 684-13334-2.

If you are of the fishing persuasion and are called by far-away places, this guide may be just the thing. It could even be useful for those who don't fish but just want to go to the more rustic—and perhaps less expensive—areas of a few countries to relax. Herein is information on fishing, of course, hotel accommodations and rates, currency exchange (subject to rapid change), clothing appropriate to the weather, fishing guides, license fees and regulations, and much more. There are about 40 nations or island areas included, with keyed maps for finding fish. Small enough for easy carrying, paperback, and inexpensive.

10. Marston, A. Norman, ed. **Encyclopedia of Angling.** London, Hamlyn Pub.; distr. Levittown, N.Y., Transatlantic Arts, 1969. 286p. illus. $15.00.

In an alphabetic arrangement, entries cover the entire field of fishing in Britain with a number of special articles, signed by the writers, about material that can not be easily abbreviated into a few lines. Well illustrated with line drawings, photos, and color plates. Fishermen are probably pretty much the same the world over, differing primarily in terminology peculiar to their languages or locales, and much of this volume will be useful to American fishermen. The differences in terminology, however, may cause some confusion.

11. Needham, Paul R. **Trout Streams**. New York, Winchester, 1969. 241p. illus. index. $8.50. LC 70-105668.

While *Trout Streams* is not a book about fishing *per se*, it is of great importance to fishermen, conservationists, and ichthyologists. It is a study of the streams themselves and their inhabitants from the viewpoint of a biologist–hence, it is a biological treatise. The data presented here are the culmination of many years of study and analysis of trout streams in both the East and the West. It begins with the trout, salmon, and grayling, following their life cycles and describing their physical structures. Their habitat is surveyed for temperature ranges, oxygen and carbon dioxide ratios, insect and crustacean population, predators, and parasites, then related to the food selections of different species of fish. Information on the propagation and management of trout and trout waters is the summary, or end result, of the study.

12. **The New Fisherman's Encyclopedia**. 2nd ed. Ed. by Ira N. Gabrielson. Harrisburg, Pa., Stackpole, 1963. 759p. illus. index. $19.95. LC 63-22468.

A companion volume to the *New Hunter's Encyclopedia*, this magnificent compendium of piscatorial knowledge presents more than most folks will ever want to know about fish and fishing. In the foreword, humorist Corey Ford says that this volume has "the what, the where, the when and the how. Everything, in fact, but the why." He then discusses the "why." There are seven major sections, beginning with game fish, both fresh and salt water varieties, divided by type such as shark, mackerel and tuna, crevalles, etc. The second section tells all about equipment and methods for fishing. Properly taught and equipped, the fisherman then learns about boats to get to fishing waters. While on the way, some thorough indoctrination is done in the theories and practices of conservation. Where to fish, when and how to fish, and miscellaneous topics round out the seven sections. Heavily illustrated: there are nine full-color plates of fish, flies, and lures in addition to the other photos and drawings. Thorough and complete, this is a lot of book for the money.

Wildlife & General

13. **The American Sportsman Treasury**. Ed. and with a preface by Jerry Mason. New York, Ridge Press & Knopf, 1971. 252p. illus. $14.95. LC 72-158810. ISBN 0-394-47296-9.

The articles in this collection are drawn mainly from the now-defunct "The American Sportsman" television series. The authors, all well-known sportsmen and frequent contributors to sports and conservation magazines, provide interesting and well-written tales of hunting, fishing, and travel in many parts of America. The outstanding color photographs and paintings by Carl Rungius depict game birds, fish, and other wild species in their natural habitats. Seldom does one find such a combination of beautiful illustrations, excellent writing, and fine typography all in one volume. This is a book for everyone–hunter, fisherman, conservationist, ecologist, artist.

14. Bauer, Erwin A. **Treasury of Big Game Animals**. New York, Outdoor Life/Harper & Row, 1972. 398p. illus. index. $12.50. LC 72-90933. SBN 06-010243-8.

This treasury is indeed a treasure for all who are interested in the large, wild animals of the world. It is not a hunting book in the usual sense, although the author was hunting with cameras and in most instances with a gun. The quantity of full-color photos (only a few are not in color) explains the price, but the collection is worth the money. The major big game animals were all photographed in their natural habitats: only Antarctica (penguins don't count) and Oceania (kangaroos don't, either) are omitted. The book is divided by continent, and the text describes habitat, the animals, and hunting conditions and methods in a general way. Excellent for the environmentalist as well as the hunter, but unfortunately, photographic information for the camera buff was not included.

15. Gregg, James. **The Sportsman's Eye**. New York, Winchester, 1971. 210p. illus. index. $6.95. LC 73-150385. ISBN 0-87691-035-5.

Of the five senses, most people dread most the thought of losing sight. The total loss of vision is not the point of Gregg's work; rather, he is concerned with the care and preservation of eyes and with getting the most out of your eyes. As a practicing optometrist and an enthusiastic outdoor sportsman, he is well qualified to instruct and advise on problems of sight. The phenomenon of sight is explained in laymen's language and compared to the visual capabilities of animals, birds, and fish. The uses and specialized purposes of optical aids (glasses, binoculars, telescopes) for outdoor conditions are thoroughly discussed. The more the optometrist knows about the activities of the sportsman, the non-sportsmen, too, the better he is able to provide the proper lenses for good eye care.

16. Murie, Olaus J. **A Field Guide to Animal Tracks.** Boston, Houghton Mifflin, 1954. 374p. illus. index. $5.95. LC 54-9602. ISBN 0-395-08037-1.

Learning to recognize tracks is frequently the only way of determining the identities of animals living in any given area, since most are shy and retiring and many are nocturnal. The guide book includes every obtainable track for animals in North America, Mexico, and Central America, plus tracks of some birds, reptiles, and a few insects. Line drawings of the animals in their habitats, of their tracks, and of their droppings–along with a brief description of the animals and their habits–result in an excellent, concise identification manual for wildlife. Conveniently small for easy carrying when hiking, hunting, or camping.

17. Ormond, Clyde. **Outdoorsman's Handbook.** New York, Outdoor Life/Dutton, 1970. 336p. illus. index. $5.95. LC 76-134237.

Clyde Ormond is recognized as an outdoor writer of the first order. This latest manual is for the outdoorsman, be he hunter, fisherman, or hiker and camper. It could very well be included in any bibliography of survival books since his "how-to" instructions are based on the assumption that the reader is unable or unwilling to buy everything he needs at the moment that the need arises. Indeed, a hiker who carried enough items to meet every eventuality would not be a hiker but the leader of a caravan. Among the many things to be made as needed are: grass or leaf beds that are both dry and comfortable; emergency needles from tin cans; jacks and hoists; survival knives; buttons, emergency whistles, shelters, and foods. Copiously illustrated with line drawings to clarify instructions, this volume is a must for everyone who gets out into the woods for an outing.

18. Raymond, Steve. **Kamloops: An Angler's Study of the Kamloops Trout.** New York, Winchester, 1971. 209p. illus. bibliog. index. $12.50. LC 71-146058. ISBN 0-87691-026-6.

Although the Kamloops is world famous as a game fish, relatively little has been written about it until this volume. The author is a journalist, but his research has been from the biological viewpoint. One interesting point is that when transplanted to warmer waters, the Kamloops loses the characteristics of the Kamloops and appears to be an ordinary rainbow trout. Management of the Kamloops as a game fish and as an important economic resource to its British Columbian habitat began seriously after World War II, and research and investigation continues. Its fame as a fighter brings fishermen from all over the world, and fishing pressure increases each year. At this time, this is undoubtedly the definitive work on this specie.

19. Taylor, Walter P. **The Deer of North America**. Harrisburg, Pa., Stackpole, and Washington, The Wildlife Management Institute, 1956. 668p. illus. bibliog. index. $12.50. LC 56-7897. ISBN 0-8117-0490-4.

Copies of this title are from the fourth printing, 1969. This is an important work, although it is not likely to be in great demand by most hunters because it is a technical, scientific study of "The White-tailed, Mule and Black-tailed Deer, Genus *Odocoileus*. Their History and Management." The time span from the beginning of research to publication was about nine years, and the study actually begins with the deer, the Indians, and the American pioneers. It is then divided for studies of the white-tail deer and the mule and black-tail deer, the latter two being closely related. There were 16 authors, all biologists and/or game management specialists. Hunting is covered as an aspect of management and as a means of thinning herds that are overpopulated for the forage available. Perhaps this book will encourage more hunters to take the time to understand deer management problems than have done so in the past.

20. Wall, Roy. **Game and Fish: From Field to Table**. San Antonio, Tex., Naylor, 1972. 132p. $4.95. LC 76-183417. ISBN 0-8111-0442-7.

Large quantities of game meat are lost each year by hunters and fishermen in the field who do not know the proper methods to prevent spoilage or the loss of flavor. Wall tells how to care for game from the time of the kill until it is placed on the table. He includes his own tried and tested recipes for different ways of preparing game and fish either at home or in camp. There is little duplication of recipes found in other books, since each gourmet or cook has his own preferences for seasoning, cooking time, or relishes. The author gives detailed instructions on dressing and caring for game, emphasizing cleanliness, cooling as quickly as possible, and the removal of damaged parts to prevent spoiling. This is a fine addition to a sportsman's cooking library, with an especially fine chapter on sauces and garnishes.

21. Wylie, Stephen R., and Stewart S. Furlong. **Key to North American Waterfowl**. Illus. by Jack R. Schroeder. Wynnewood, Pa.,

Livingston Pub. Co., 1972. 31p. illus. index. $2.98. LC 72-6951. ISBN 0-87098-047-5.

There have been guides to waterfowl published in the past and there will undoubtedly be more in the future. They are very much alike in content, are usually small and paperback, and do not have a very long life span if used frequently. This edition gives common name, technical name, ranges of lengths and weights, flight patterns, and food and habitat preferences. There is also a color coding to indicate each of the four major flyways and the likelihood of seeing each specie in each flyway. Symbols for the latter are "A" for accidental, "U" for uncommon, "R" for rare, and "C" for common. In use, the black duck is coded common in the Atlantic flyway, uncommon in the Mississippi, rare in the central, and accidental in the Pacific flyway. Both sexes of each specie are shown in full color, and two additional silhouettes are shown–one in flight, the other at the time of take-off from water. The most interesting feature of this booklet is the material on which it is printed, an opaque plastic that is waterproof, grease-proof, and washable. It can be carried in foul weather (no pun intended), and can be cleaned easily if dropped in the mud. Do not use hot water. The toughness of the plastic should result in a much longer life with hard usage than that of the paper editions.

Chapter 3

HUNTING

General

22. Cone, Arthur L., Jr. **The Complete Guide to Hunting.** New York, Macmillan, 1970. 335p. illus. index. $6.95. LC 70-119124.

Cone presents an overall survey of all kinds of hunting on the North American continent, with major emphasis on hunting in the 48 contiguous states. One of the most outstanding parts of the book is the writer's defense of hunters and hunting. "It has always been the sportsman who has come through with the hard cash required to make conservation something more than an altruistic ideal or a sad joke. The eighty million dollars spent by hunters on licenses alone is a bigger contribution to conservation than all the chitchat of self-styled moralists who look up from their steak to ask, 'How could you kill one of God's own creatures?' " If those who condemn hunters and hunting would only do some unbiased study on hunting, game management, and conservation and could intelligently accept scientific fact from research, there would be less controversy–or perhaps some people would prefer that wildlife starve rather than be taken by the hunter.

23. Dalrymple, Byron W. **Complete Guide to Hunting Across North America.** New York, Outdoor Life/Harper & Row, 1970. 848p. illus. maps. $10.00. LC 70-115429. ISBN 0-87468-048-4.

A massive work of tremendous value, the guide surveys hunting possibilities of North America, north of the Rio Grande. Hawaii is excluded since it is not in North America, even though it is a state. The volume is divided into nine regions, with Alaska and the Canadian provinces grouped together as one region. Groupings do not necessarily follow the divisions generally accepted for other purposes, since they depend on the types of game found in a region. Within each region a state-by-state analysis is made of the hunting available and its quality, and public hunting areas are located on a map. After a general statement on hunting in each state, specific birds and animals are discussed. Data are precise, yet are general enough for use year after year. Exact figures for game from census surveys are not given; the guide is not designed for only the current year, as is the 1973 *Winchester Hunter's Handbook*. At the end are two directories: one is for shooting preserves, with name, address, and phone number of the manager, and types of game available; the second is a hunting area locator, an alphabetic listing of public hunting areas nationwide.

24. Elman, Robert. **The Great American Shooting Prints**. New York, Knopf, 1972. 1v.(unpaged). plates. $25.00. LC 79-183379. ISBN 0-394-47178-4.

Each of the 72 plates is a full-color reproduction of an original painting concerning some form of hunting in America. The brief text accompanying each plate tells something of the artist and describes the action taking place in the painting or places it in historical perspective. For the most part, the original paintings are in museums, and many are by well-known artists: Catlin, Audubon, Miller, Bierstadt, Remington, Russell, Homer, Seltzer, Hunt, and many others. Each page is approximately 12 x 16 in. with prints varying in size, proportionate to the original. An outstanding production!

25. Holman, Dennis, with Eric Rundgren. **Inside Safari Hunting**. New York, Putnam, 1970. 296p. photos. bibliog. index. $6.95. LC 76-99285. ISBN 0-399-10443-7.

"White hunter" Rundgren is the subject and source for African hunting experiences spanning a period of some 40 years. The prologue inquires into the origin of the safari traditions and the question of why hunters hunt. Hunters' attitudes have changed over the past century: the idea that massive kills were necessary, desirable, or sportsmanlike has evolved into a very selective hunting for trophies. This emphasis on achieving new records is, in a sense, an extension of the spirit of competition; it is most beneficial for conservation, since it removes the largest and possibly the oldest animals from the herds. There have been and still are scientific expeditions that hunt to fill collections in museums or to provide research capabilities with hides, skulls, and skeletons, but these are very restricted hunts. Rundgren has served as guide for all sorts of hunters.

26. Ormond, Clyde. **Complete Book of Hunting.** Rev. and updated ed. New York, Outdoor Life/Harper & Row, 1972. 432p. illus. index. $6.95. LC 77-169126. ISBN 0-87468-009-3.

When one sees a book called "Complete book of . . ." the initial reaction is one of suspicion and disbelief. With hundreds, perhaps thousands, of volumes available in a given field, how can one small volume be a "complete" anything, even if it is by such a respected authority and writer as Ormond? The point, of course, is definition. The first edition of this title appeared in 1962. Ormond's revised work on hunting seems to include all North American big game and most small game and birds, although there are some omissions. Information provided on hunting, clothing, food, packs and packing, horses, and guns is succinct and is based on the author's broad personal experiences. Economy is important to most hunters and Ormond makes an excellent distinction between "economy" and "cheapness" by telling of five "cheap" hunts for elk, with no results, and one successful trip that cost as much as the preceding five. Clothing and gear that is rather expensive may be more economical than cheap equipment combined with several days of discomfort or sickness. Illustrations include both drawings (by Douglas Allen) and photos. The whole book is well done, is well illustrated, has good information on Boone & Crockett Club measurement requirements for records, and is attractive and well bound. It is worth the price for any library, but the adjective "complete" is still bothersome.

27. Ripley, Aiden Lassell. **Sporting Etchings.** Commentary by Dana S. Lamb. Barre, Mass., Barre Publishers, 1970. 91p. illus. $17.50. LC 72-111105. SBN 8271-7005-X.

Aiden Lassell Ripley was an artist, especially a water colorist, until his death in 1969. These 40 etchings of upland and water fowl were done, at least partially, during the Depression years at a time when artists were not able to sell much of their work. Besides being an artist, Ripley was a hunter, preferring upland birds, and a fisherman for trout and salmon. Each etching is accompanied by a commentary in the form of a brief explanation of the scene depicted or by a brief story that could have been told at the time of the etching. Reproductions of the etchings are from the originals and the quality of reproduction is excellent, with each fine, delicate line appearing sharp and clear.

28. Strung, Norman. **The Hunter's Almanac**. New York, Macmillan, 1971. 240p. illus. $4.95. LC 74-144149.

As the title suggests, *The Hunter's Almanac* is in almanac format giving precise data for each game animal. Strung provides name, size, identifying characteristics, distribution figures, and pertinent information on habitat and habits of each animal. Like any almanac, this one is designed to give the most information in the least space, with very little room for trivia. Articles two to ten pages long are included on general topics such as hunting dogs, guns, guides, etc. Hunting seasons for various species in each state are shown in quick reference charts. *The Hunter's Almanac* is a companion volume to Dan Morris and Norman Strung's *The Fisherman's Almanac*; it has the same arrangement as the earlier volume.

Big Game

29. Anderson, Luther A. **How to Hunt Whitetail Deer**. New York, Funk & Wagnalls, 1968. 180p. illus. $5.95. LC 68-21717.

Whitetail deer are found in greatest numbers east of the Rockies, and are probably the most hunted big game species in the contiguous 48 states. Information on guns and ammunition, other gear, habits of whitetails, care of meat, camping, and much more is included here. An excellent guide for the novice; nevertheless, some adaptation must be made for specific locales and special problems, since it is impossible to cover everything one might need to know.

30. Laycock, George. **The Deer Hunter's Bible**. Rev. ed. New York, Doubleday, 1971. 154p. illus. $1.95pa. LC 70-139454. ISBN 0-385-01328-0pa.

Deer, of one species or another, is the most widespread of all the big game animals in North America. East of the Rocky Mountains the whitetail is most common–it is found even within the city limits of New York City. There are whitetail in some areas of the West, but mule deer and blacktail are more common. Laycock discusses deer hunting from A to Z; the species, their habits and habitats, rifles, shotguns, and bows used in taking deer, and proper care in dressing the animal and caring for and cooking venison. Well illustrated with photographs and drawings, this is an excellent guide to the sport, especially for the beginner.

31. Mattis, George. **Whitetail: Fundamentals and Fine Points for the Hunter**. New York, Outdoor Life/World, 1969. 273p. illus. index. $6.95. LC 71-89820. ISBN 0-87468-045-X.

While hunting is the main theme of this volume, another very important part is observation and study of nature—woods, plants, wildlife. Hunting information is quite similar to that given by Anderson in *How to Hunt Whitetail Deer*, but Mattis' work might be described as being more philosophical in approach. Nature study is, of course, practical as well as aesthetic, since observing plants, animals, and birds may give a clue to the presence of deer. On the other hand, they also tell deer that man is present in the woods.

32. O'Connor, Jack. **Big Game Hunts**. New York, Dutton, 1963. 415p. illus. $4.95. LC 63-8069.

A prolific writer, O'Connor has gathered together his stories from *Outdoor Life* magazine where he has been gun editor for a great many years. He has hunted all over the world and has experiences to tell that make exciting reading: African safaris, tigers in India, sheep, goats, moose, and other North American big game. Well illustrated, this is good for evenings by the fire. Other volumes by the same author are listed elsewhere in this guide.

33. Robinson, Rollo S. **Shots at Mule Deer**. New York, Winchester, 1972. 209p. illus. $8.95. LC 70-159429. ISBN 0-87691-040-1.

Mule deer are western big game, and hunting season is the time of mass migration—of hunters. Too many, unfortunately, know too little about muleys, too little about hunting and camping, and too little about rifles and shooting. Robinson's book can, if taken to heart, remedy some of these lacks; he covers the mule deer from conception to consumption. A reasonable knowledge of habits and habitat is necessary since there is little to be gained by hunting where deer probably aren't. The author's discussion of rifles suitable for mule deer is thorough and sensible. Any of the guns mentioned will and have taken deer, even though some are really too weak for the average hunter, but it is the man behind the gun that makes the difference. Laws in some states determine the minimum standards for big game rifles. Hunting methods, clothing, footwear, and camping advice are all based on many years of experience by this westerner. After the deer is down comes the task of skinning, butchering, and cooking the meat. Some recipes are included, but more varieties of preparation will be found in cookbooks like Roy Wall's (entry 20). There are instructions for those who want to try their hand at mounting the head.

34. Roosevelt, Theodore. **Ranch Life and the Hunting Trail**. Illus. by Frederic Remington. New York, Winchester; distr. New York, McGraw-Hill, 1970. 186p. illus. $10.00. LC 72-81762.

This book is primarily about ranching in the Dakotas around the turn of the century; it is included here because its last four chapters discuss hunting elk, big-horn sheep, mountain goat, deer, and antelope. Roosevelt was almost as famous for his hunting expeditions, both in Africa and in America, as he was for his term in the White House. He was an outspoken conservationist and a leader in the move to create national parks and wilderness areas. Most readers will enjoy his writings as a picture of a time when life was much simpler in many ways, but more difficult so far as comfort and labor-saving conveniences are concerned.

35. Sell, Francis E. **The Deer Hunter's Guide**. Harrisburg, Pa., Stackpole, 1964. 192p. illus. index. $5.00. LC 64-14891.

Deer, of one species or another, are the most heavily hunted of all North American big game, yet with good game management programs in most states they continue to survive and thrive; they have even been replanted successfully in areas that have not had deer for many years because of overhunting. They are here to stay and hunters need to learn as much as they can about good hunting practices to ensure the continuance of their sport. Sell has hunted whitetail, blacktail, muleys, and others with rifles and shotguns. He speaks from experience when giving advice on gun selection and loads, hunting methods used, and how to care for the deer after the kill. The photographs were made by him, and all the deer kills described were also made by him. He debunks some of the stories of long-range shots on running deer as they crossed a small clearing by timing different gaits of deer with a stop watch, showing mathematically that some of the tales, if true, were really miraculous.

36. Strung, Norman. **Tactics and Guns for Hunting All North American Deer**. Philadelphia, Lippincott, 1973. illus. $7.95.

There are a great many books around on deer hunting in general or on one specie or another. Although there is some duplication of information, each one also contains much that is not duplicated, primarily personal experiences. Terrain varies widely and deer do not always react the way one expects, so the experience of one hunter may be diametrically opposed to that of another. There is considerable discussion of deer and their habits and habitats in this volume, with a frequent reminder that the animal being hunted may not conform to the proper habit and may fool the hunter. Mule deer will sometimes stop in answer to a yell or a whistle to seek its source, but Strung tells of one that hadn't read the rules and kept on running. There is also a general discussion of guns and ammunition and bow hunting for deer, but perhaps the most important and hard-hitting section is on deer management. The simplified illustration of a management area being mismanaged is clear and strong. Unfortunately, the mismanagement is too often *demanded* by well-meaning but ill-informed citizens, including hunters. This section, at least, should be read by all who oppose the management practices of the fish and game specialists in the various states to learn that the major problem is not the management of deer herds, but rather the management of people. An off-print of this chapter should be given to each purchaser of a deer hunting license.

Small Game

37. Anderson, Luther A. **How to Hunt American Small Game**. New York, Funk & Wagnalls, 1969. 167p. illus. $5.95. LC 68-56454.

Small game is available to the hunter in most parts of the nation throughout most of the year. Anderson discusses hunting techniques, guns and ammunition, and clothing for those in pursuit of small animals such as squirrels and rabbits, upland birds, waterfowl of all types, and the red fox. Boys usually learn to hunt small game and later in life look back on those years as the best, even though they may hunt bigger game now. Readable and reliable as a guide, especially for the novice. Illustrations are 12 photos of hunting situations.

Birds

38. Becker, A. C., Jr. **Game and Bird Calling**. New York, A. S. Barnes, 1972. 146p. illus. bibliog. index. $7.95. LC 79-168368. ISBN 0-498-07891-4.

An active hunter himself, Becker discusses the many different game sounds, game habits, and the art of game calling. He tells how to call the various species and explains why and how they respond to the calls. It takes a lot of practice to produce the proper sounds; hitting a "clunker," or a sour note will drive the quarry away, sometimes at top speed. Some records are available to help the beginner learn the correct sounds and calling methods.

39. Becker, A. C., Jr. **Waterfowl in the Marshes**. New York, A. S. Barnes, 1970. 155p. illus. index. $7.50. LC 69-13030. ISBN 0-498-06948-6.

As an active sportsman and sportswriter, Becker writes about the waterfowl hunting that he loves and gives instructions to the amateur, reminiscences to the experienced, and helpful information to all. Waterfowl hunting is not a sport for the indolent or for one who dislikes early rising, physical exertion, or the discomforts of the wind, the cold, and the wet. All of these are obstacles that the successful duck and goose hunter experiences. Waterfowl hunting methods probably vary less from place to place than do those of most other forms of hunting, so this volume is not limited in usefulness to any one locale. The author discusses decoys ("Falsie in the Marsh"), gun handling ("It's Polite to Point"), estimating distances ("Whites of Their Eyes"), proper clothing ("Clothes Make the Man"), and safety ("Perils of Pauline"). Even the lazy hunter could easily be inspired to hunt with the techniques outlined in this book.

40. Duffey, David Michael. **Bird-Hunting Know-How**. Princeton, Van Nostrand, 1968. 192p. illus. $5.95. LC 68-8090.

The personal experiences of the author deal primarily with the many facets of bird hunting in the eastern and mid-western states. Guns, dogs, safety, hunting clubs and preserves, and hunting clothing are all given practical attention. Much of his experience can be adapted for areas and habitats not mentioned specifically, especially when hunting the same species in other parts of the nation.

41. Evans, George Bird. **The Upland Shooting Life**. New York, Knopf, 1971. 301p. illus. index. $10.00. LC 72-161404. ISBN 0-394-47295-0.

This is the personal, revealing philosophy of a hunter who is more concerned with his dogs, fair sportsmanship, and the ways of grouse, quail, pheasant, and woodcock then he is with the number of birds brought to bag. Then, at day's end, all is complete with a cozy fire and companionship. A philosophical approach such as this comes only with a lifetime of hunting and much thought.

42. Foster, William Harnden. **New England Grouse Shooting**. New York, Scribner's, 1942; repr. Scribner's, 1970. 193p. illus. $12.50. LC 42-25613. ISBN 0-684-12413-0.

A native of New England, Foster was both an artist and naturalist as well as a hunter of the native grouse, known also as partridge or pa'tridge. His illustrations, in pen and ink, are exquisitely detailed. Grouse hunting, as he learned it from his father, is both an art and a sport, with the pleasures of being out-of-doors in a crisp fall morning as an added attraction. Guns suitable for these upland birds in the New England cover, dogs for hunting, and the proper clothing are all discussed. The final chapter, "A Lesson in Grouse Shooting," is written as an event involving a veteran and a novice, complete with dialogue in dialect. The veteran gives instructions on what and what not to do, the beginner tries his best, and the veteran responds with helpful criticism. A reading of the lesson is much more effective than the usual straightforward detailing of instructions. Printed with distinctive type on high-quality paper, this is a beautiful volume to own and to read.

43. Hill, Gene. **A Hunter's Fireside Book**. Drawings by Milton C. Weber. New York, Winchester, 1972. 162p. illus. $7.95. LC 72-79359. ISBN 0-87691-076-2.

Books made up of columns from magazines are sometimes successful, sometimes not. This collection is one of the "is" group. Reminiscences, thoughts, ideas, the essence of an outdoorsman's mind and inner being make enjoyable reading for others with like feelings and interests. Some of the thoughts remind us that we all have a bit of Charley Brown in us—natural-born losers, at one time or another. When the quail rise, there is too much brush; when ducks settle to decoys, the sun is in the wrong place. Hill's tales of dogs, ducks, birds, and guns provide amusement and detail activities that all sportsmen can identify as statements of their own experiences.

44. Hinman, Bob. **The Golden Age of Shotgunning**. New York, Winchester, 1971. 175p. illus. $8.95. LC 72-159432. ISBN 0-87691-043-6.

Until the last third of the nineteenth century, America was predominantly a rifleman's country. Changing technology, however, coupled with a bountiful supply of game birds, ushered in the era of the market hunters who supplied hotels, restaurants, and markets with huge quantities of ducks, geese, pigeon, quail, prairie chickens, and many other species. Few game laws existed, and bag limits were determined only by the hunter's skill. In retrospect, it was a time of much abuse of wildlife resources, but at the time a depleted bird population was unthinkable. The golden age was of relatively short duration, but it set the stage for many later developments in game management, and it also affected shotgun development.

45. Waterman, Charles. **Hunting Upland Birds**. New York, Winchester, 1972. 311p. illus. index. $8.95. LC 72-79362. ISBN 0-87691-078-9.

Upland game birds can be found reasonably close to almost any point on the North American continent; therefore, there are a great many hunters who hunt birds at some time during the year, even if it is incidental to the hunting of other small game. Nine species and their subspecies are studied, with information on their habits, habitats, and the hunting procedure and advice needed to be successful in the hunt. The author's personal experiences—both good and bad—are included.

Varmints

46. Mermon, Dick. **Crow Shooting Secrets**. New York, Winchester, 1970. 149p. illus. index. $5.95. LC 79-127957. ISBN 0-87691-021-5.

Crow shooting is a year-round sport in almost any part of the nation, since these wily pests live in all parts and do not migrate. Very intelligent and wary, crows are difficult to approach and difficult to lure within range of a scattergun unless the hunter knows his stuff. Mermon and associates have studied and hunted crows for a long time and now reveal secrets to enable others to enjoy the sport to the fullest. A knowledge of decoys and their placement, crow calls, blinds, camouflage clothing, guns, and specialty items are all essential to the successful shooter. Crows are found in every part of the countryside and even inside New York City's Central Park—but don't try hunting them there. As a damager of crops and a raider of game bird nests, crows are a nuisance to both farmers and sportsmen, and a crow hunter is more likely to be welcome on a farm when crow hunting than when in pursuit of some other game. This is an excellent sport at any time, but especially during the off-season. Mermon's methods are clear and explicit.

Hunting Dogs, Training and Use

47. Duffey, David Michael. **Hunting Dog Know-How**. New York, Winchester, 1972. 182p. illus. index. $5.95. LC 72-79487. ISBN 0-87691-081-9.

Duffey dotes on dogs—he must, to hunt with them, train them, and write about the different breeds and purposes of hunting canines. For most upland bird hunters or waterfowlers, a well-trained dog is a very important part of a working team. In this volume, Duffey examines the most popular breeds, their specialties, and their problems, and advises on the selection, care, and training that are essential for best development of the hunter's companion. Some hunters prefer to buy a dog that is already trained, and for some men, this may be the best way to go. Others prefer to do their own training, so a thorough set of lessons is provided to train pointers, setters, spaniels, Labradors, Chesapeakes, and many others. Perhaps there should be a companion volume to help train people to be good dog owners and companions. After all, companionship works both ways, and some men are not fit companions for even a dog.

48. Duffey, David Michael. **Hunting Hounds**. New York, Winchester, 1972. 184p. illus. index. $5.95. LC 72-188593. ISBN 0-87691-062-2.

Duffey attributes the dearth of literature about hounds to the fact that hound men are doers and talkers, not writers or readers. Those who know the most about the subject, therefore, pass on their knowledge only to their friends and fellow hunters by conversation, and the outsider is left outside. Dividing hounds into two main divisions—those that trail by scent and those that trail by sight—the author then subdivides by species, breeds, types, or whatever, and goes into history, training, and selection of hunting hounds. It all becomes rather confusing at times and close attention must be given to the histories. When is a foxhound not a foxhound? When it is a coonhound. Then there are those that hunt wolves, coyotes, bear, boar, deer, rabbits, and the big cats. Each type has its special purpose, select ancestry, and training. The whole subject is fascinating. Duffey hunted in both the North and the South with many hound chasers in preparation for this book, and he has included many excellent photos of dogs in action.

49. Falk, John R. **The Practical Hunter's Dog Book**. New York, Winchester, 1971. 314p. illus. index. $8.95. LC 70-159426. ISBN 0-87691-037-1.

The choosing and training of a hunting dog is a many-sided problem, affected by type or types of hunting to be done, varieties of landscape to be worked, and the personality and likes of the hunter. An experienced hunter and trainer of dogs, Falk discusses the different breeds of hunting animals and their histories, personalities, and special qualifications, in order to enable hunters to make the right choice among hunting companions. The author has owned a kennel and has trained dogs for others and has, no doubt, encountered a wide variety of problems in matching dogs with men for the best relationship between the two.

Chapter 4

FISHING

General

50. Evanoff, Vlad. **Another 1001 Fishing Tips and Tricks.** New York, Harper & Row, 1970. 206p. illus. index. $5.95. LC 70-95953. ISBN 0-06-011187-9.

No actual count was made to verify the figure in the title—we'll take the author's word for it. Tips and tricks there are, however, in abundance, and all are designed to help the fisherman better enjoy his sport and to improve his chances of bringing home more and bigger fish at the end of the day. Please note the phrase "improve his chances" since nothing is 100% guaranteed. Useful to both the fresh- and the salt-water fisherman, the tips are brief and pointed. It is reminiscent of the old timer who teaches a beginner not with long, cultured lectures, but rather with something like, "Why'n'cha change to a worm 'n' fish a little deeper." Illustrated with line drawings.

51. Evanoff, Vlad. **A Complete Guide to Fishing.** New York, Crowell, 1961. 208p. illus. index. $4.50. LC 61-7618. ISBN 0-690-20691-7.

Fishing has been going on since the beginning of time, but the reasons for fishing have changed over the centuries, at least in the more progressive countries. Originally fish were simply food, an essential element in survival. Now, however, while fishing is still done for food, both individually and commercially, the chief purpose in angling is for sport, rest, and relaxation. From the barefoot boy with a cane pole, bottle cork, and makeshift hook to the sophisticate with elegant rods, reels, special clothing, and other expensive appurtenances, the goal of pleasure is the same. Most fishermen begin with the simple necessities, so Evanoff has covered the basics in all forms of sport fishing—hand line, hook, cork, and sinker through deep-sea fishing. The general discussion covers baits, lures, and types of fish and tackle, although specific brands and costs are avoided. Print is large for easy reading, line drawings are clear, and presentation is aimed at the novice. A section on making your own tackle is very interesting.

52. Fichter, George S., and Phil Francis. **A Guide to Fresh and Salt-Water Fishing**. Ed. by Herbert S. Zim. New York, Golden Press, 1965. 160p. illus. index. $4.95PLB; $1.25pa. LC 64-8043.

One of the Golden Handbooks, this is a handy pocket or tacklebox size reference volume on all kinds of fishing. In a very concise format, identification and a statement are provided for 95 salt-water species and/or groups, seven species of salmon that are both salt- and fresh-water inhabitants, and 30 fresh-water fishes. Full-color illustrations are used throughout the book. Baits, lures, tackle, accessories, and equipment are covered in wide array, along with instructions on how to rig for fishing under varying conditions, how to cast with the different types of outfits, how to set the hook, and how to "read" a stream or lake to determine the best possibilities for success. There is little of depth here, but it is excellent as a convenient reference.

53. McNally, Tom, ed. **Tom McNally's Fishermen's Bible**. Chicago, Follett, 1970. 321p. illus. $4.95pa. LC 73-99591. ISBN 0-695-81096-0.

Another "Bible"—and if we all lived by all the bibles available, it would be smooth sailing for everyone. McNally, a regular feature article contributor to *Outdoor Life* and *Field and Stream* magazines has collected a number of articles on the "how" and "where" of fishing and tells how to use baits and artificial lures. There is an abundance of useful, statistical information on organizations, conservation and state conservation departments, and fishing records, and there is a directory of manufacturers of fishing tackle and equipment. Canada and the Bahamas are included since both are fished regularly by residents of the United States.

54. Morris, Dan, and Norman Strung. **The Fisherman's Almanac**. New York, Macmillan, 1970. 231p. $4.95. LC 70-93179.

Fishermen's almanacs and fishermen's calendars! Some sportsmen swear by them, while others swear at them, depending on whether or not the fishing trip was successful. The validity of an almanac can not be exclusively determined, however, by the success of a trip, since the right bait or lure, the right place (one with fish) and the right method (know-how) are also necessary. Scientific research has shown that fish react in a fairly predictable manner to changes in barometric pressure, changes in water level and temperature, and changes in season that alter both temperature and sunlight. An almanac, then, is based on known seasonal changes and past fishing success, with guiding information on what to look for in weather changes and how to apply the information. The present almanac presents the basic information that the fisherman should know to determine the best possibilities for a successful fishing trip, and lists the best known species of fish for the 50 states including sea species for the coastal states. In a dictionary format are given Latin names, common names, sizes, range, fishing methods, general information, and taste, which ranges from inedible to delicious. There are also tables showing legal fishing seasons for the various species in all states.

55. Poltroon, Milford ("Stanley"). **How to Fish Good**. New York, Winchester, 1971. 128p. illus. $2.95pa. LC 78-163779. ISBN 0-87691-051-7.

A mess of hilarity put together by Dave Bascom, editor of the *Wretched Mess News*, *How to Fish Good* is zanier than Ed Zern's *To Hell with Fishing*. Poltroon (even the name is an indication of things to come) touches all bases from weather forecasting, lying, spawning, psychiatry, art and snobbery, through gambling, history, and spelling. If there is a serious thought expressed it is well camouflaged and is not likely to be found. No collection on fishing, or other sporting events, is complete without this piece of tomfoolery.

56. Waterman, Charles F. **Modern Fresh and Salt Water Fly Fishing**. New York, Winchester, 1972. 368p. illus. index. $8.95. LC 70-188598. ISBN 0-87691-063-0.

The author discusses his experiences on many fishing trips, describing techniques with fly tackle that have been successful or not so successful. Flies, methods of presentation, and length and weight of rods and lines vary with species, fresh or salt water. Recommendations are made as a guide to the beginner. Matching line to rod is essential for good casting and the capacity of the reel is determined to a great extent by the fish to be caught.

57. Willock, Colin, ed. **The Penguin Guide to Fishing**. Baltimore, Penguin, 1966. 368p. illus. index. $1.95pa. ISBN 0-14-046112-4.

First published as the *ABC of Fishing* under the editorship of Andre Deutch, this is a composite publication with parts written by eight different contributors. The fishing methods, fish, and waters are British, although some of the techniques described can be applied elsewhere. Divided into three parts: coarse fishing refers to fresh-water non-game species; game fishing concerns the taking of trout and salmon; and sea fishing, of course, is salt-water angling.

58. Wulff, Lee. **Fishing with Lee Wulff.** Ed. by Edward C. Janes. New York, Knopf, 1972. 348p. illus. $8.95. LC 78-171117. ISBN 0-394-46920-8.

Author of five books about fishing, Winchester's Outdoorsman of the Year, and frequent contributor to sporting journals, Lee Wulff has packed more fishing experiences into his years than several ordinary fishermen will in their combined lifetimes. Fly fishing is his specialty, whether the quarry is the trout of small streams or the mighty marlin or tackle-busting tarpon. The book, divided into five parts with a total of 49 chapters, treats fishing with a fly in considerable depth. Part four, on rods, tackle, and technique, is really the basis for understanding and appreciating the action and instructions provided in the other parts. Illustrated with photographs of Wulff in action, this volume is a comprehensive text for the light tackle enthusiast.

Salt-Water Fishing

59. Brooks, Joe. **Salt Water Game Fishing**. New York, Harper & Row, 1968. 288p. illus. index. $6.95. LC 67-28829. ISBN 0-06-070547-7.

The fish discussed by the writer run from five pounds to over 1,000 pounds, and struggles to land the big ones have been known to last for hours. This is fishing for big game—a sport beyond the experience of most land-locked fishermen, who strive to land fish in the two- to five-pound range. Brooks is an internationally known fisherman, writer, and TV sports personality. He discusses 25 species of salt-water game fish, numerous subspecies, the tackle and bait required, sizes, records, location, and many other facets of the sport while describing, play-by-play, some of the catches made by him, by his friends, or by fishing guides. The major part of the fishing action takes place in North and Central American waters of the Atlantic, Pacific, or Caribbean, which is not necessarily as far beyond the reach of many fishermen as they might think. The appendix lists records, clubs, and regulations.

60. Cadieux, Charles L. **Introduction to Ocean Fishing**. Harrisburg, Pa., Stackpole, 1972. 192p. illus. bibliog. index. $5.95. LC 72-6669. ISBN 0-8117-0917-5.

From the increasing quantity of books on salt-water fishing it appears that with more leisure time and rising incomes there are more fishermen turning to the ocean for sport. While there is little in this volume that cannot be found elsewhere, the contents are entirely satisfactory for those who choose this book over another. The first-timer always has questions about costs of hiring a boat for a day or more, tackle costs and needs, and what the fisherman should expect from the boat owner. Currency of information, then, is an important feature of this book.

61. Cannon, Raymond. **How to Fish the Pacific Coast: A Manual for Salt Water Fishermen**. 3rd ed. Menlo Park, Calif., Lane Books, 1967. 160p. illus. index. $2.95pa. LC 67-15740. ISBN 0-376-06363-7pa.

Salt-water fishing requires a different body of knowledge, different tackle, and different lures from fresh-water fishing. In many ways, it is a whole new world, and even the east and west coasts differ. Cannon's book is a general survey of the fishing on the Pacific Coast from piers, in the surf, or from small boats. Variations in tactics required to catch the salt-water species are included. It is primarily a guide for the beginner, and the list of 202 coastal fishes with detailed descriptions and ranges will be most helpful.

62. Helm, Thomas. **Fishing Southern Salt Waters**. New York, Dodd, 1972. 393p. illus. index. $10.00. LC 70-169735. ISBN 0-396-06455-8.

Not a "how-to," "where-to," or "when-to" book, but just a good collection of interesting fishing stories for good reading and relaxing. Even the "why" of fishing is omitted–if you have to ask, then you probably wouldn't understand the answer.

63. Holm, Don. **Fishing the Pacific: An Angler's Guide to Pacific Marine Fishes**. New York, Winchester, 1972. 241p. illus. index. $6.95. LC 72-79361. ISBN 0-87691-044-4.

Approximately one-half of this work is text concerning fishing methods, gear, general identification of fishes, species, and edibility. The second half, following a glossary of terms, is an identification handbook quite similar in format to other handbooks and field guides. The index, arranged by common name, must be used to locate the desired fish. Each entry has a black and white drawing with common name(s), technical name, range, size, value (as bait or food, or its commercial use), and description.

64. MacKellar, Jean Scott. **Hawaii Goes Fishing**. Rutland, Vt., Tuttle, 1968. 160p. illus. glossary. $3.50. LC 68-29547. ISBN 0-8048-0234-3.

This is the only volume in this guide that is dedicated exclusively to fishing in our fiftieth state. With few fresh-water streams or lakes, most fishing is in salt water around the islands, and most is for the smaller fish caught from shore, by diving, or from small boats a short distance off-shore. Many of the techniques described are those used by Hawaiians for centuries and involve the use of hand-made nets and spears. Hawaiians often make fishing a community affair whenever a large school of desirable fish is spotted. The fish are driven into a cove where they can be surrounded by large nets, then everyone helps pull in the net and all share in the catch. Fish are referred to by their Hawaiian names, and many of the fishing terms are also Hawaiian; all are listed in the glossary at the back of the book. Octopus, eel, crab, and lobster are included as fair game for the fisherman. The author is Mrs. Ernest J. Sneidman in private life.

65. Moss, Frank T. **Successful Ocean Game Fishing**. Camden, Me., International Marine Publishing Co., 1971. 245p. illus. index. $12.50. LC 72-132081. ISBN 0-87742-013-0.

Bluefin tuna, sailfish, marlin, and sharks are a few of the big denizens of the deep that are the prey of the ocean fisherman. The successful angler for these large species has much to learn about tackle, boats, and fishing methods; this is a world totally apart from the fresh-water fishing that most people know best. Sport fishing boats have evolved from makeshift pleasure or working craft to the highly specialized, completely equipped rig in use today. In much the same manner, tackle and methods have changed with experience, research, and modern materials. Moss, with selections by several other writers/fishermen, examines the wide field of ocean fishing, relating experiences and giving advice to help others do better in the sport. There are proper ways to rig various types of bait, such as mullet and balao, that will present them in a desirable manner to the quarry. An understanding of basic navigation and navigational instruments could be a life-or-death matter in an emergency. Boats, navigation, and a thorough introduction to fishing are all here.

66. Mundus, Frank, and Bill Wisner. **Sportfishing for Sharks**. New York, Macmillan, 1971. 380p. illus. index. $12.95. LC 69-12177.

As the title suggests, this excellent book on a tough sport discusses every aspect of sharks: what they are like, when they attack, where they can be found, how to lure them, and how to hook, fight, and land them. In recent years there has been an increase in the interest in sharks, both as targets for fishermen and as objects of study by such researchers as Jacques Cousteau. There are many species of sharks, including some very small ones, but the ones of most interest to Mundus and Wisner are the porbeagle, blue, tiger, mako, and white. The white is the one most commonly considered a maneater. Techniques vary with each species; for success, both the boats and the fishing tackle used must be suited to this specialized sport. Even after the end of the fight a shark in a boat, if not properly handled, can be very dangerous. Instructions are presented on how to preserve, dress and butcher the shark as well as how to process and wear shark leather.

67. Sand, George X. **Salt-Water Fly Fishing**. New York, Knopf, 1969. 321p. illus. index. $8.95. LC 74-79319. ISBN 0-394-44364-0.

Fly fishing for salt-water fish is aimed primarily at the smaller species (smaller in a relative sense, that is), although large fish are caught, too. Bonefish, sea bass, barracuda, tarpon, and other species of the same ilk are most sought because they can be found in small inlets, in shallow areas, and near beaches. This kind of fishing does not require large boats and heavy tackle and is within the financial reach of most anglers. On the other hand, sharks, the large billfish, jewfish, and many other giants have been hooked and landed on fly equipment. (See Lee Wulff's work on salt-water fly fishing.) Sand does an excellent study of the sport with information on tackle, lures, and tying of flies.

68. Scharff, Robert. **Standard Handbook of Salt-Water Fishing**. Rev. and updated ed. New York, Crowell, 1966. 374p. illus. index. $8.95. LC 66-25435. ISBN 0-690-76926-1.

Almost everything that a salt-water fisherman might want to know about his sport can be found here. As some insurors insure a person from birth to death, so Scharff leads the fisherman from tidal movements through caring for the fish after it is landed. All forms of fishing (still, trolling, casting), all kinds of tackle (heavy, medium, or light), and all manner of fish commonly taken from the briny are encountered herein. One chapter is devoted to the care and repair of tackle, a very important matter because of the corrosive effect of salt water on some materials. Specific information on fishing the Atlantic, Pacific, Southern, and Gulf of Mexico coasts have been contributed by experts resident in each area. A listing of world records is interesting, but it is now seven years old and may be in need of revision.

69. Whitaker, Ralph R. **Song of the Outriggers: Big Game Fishing on the Ocean Surface**. St. Louis, Mo., Fireside Books, 1968. 311p. illus. index. $9.50. LC 68-20946.

The Caribbean is the setting for most of Whitaker's fishing stories, with the Bahamas receiving the greatest attention. These first-person tales cover a lot of territory—fish, turtles, sponges, tackle, boats, records, clubs, even American history and a bit about prohibition. At times the reader feels overwhelmed by the wide-ranging comments on so many topics, and at other times wonders about the inclusion of the minute details of each event, which tend to hide the main line of thought. There is a great deal of useful information for the salt-water fisherman, but some of it may be a little difficult to sort out. A glossary of big game fishing terms is added as an appendix, as is a list of world records as they stood in November, 1967.

70. Woolner, Frank. **Modern Saltwater Sport Fishing**. New York, Crown, 1972. 319p. illus. bibliog. index. LC 72-84308. ISBN 0-517-500388.

Surf casting, fishing from the jetty, fly fishing in the tidewaters, and going for the big ones are all part of salt-water fishing. Woolner's book is comprehensive in coverage of all phases of the sport, up-to-date on tackle, techniques, and locations. It is well illustrated to match the text. This one is better for those with some experience, but it will do well for the novice if he has an experienced friend to help out in the beginning.

Fresh-Water Fishing

GENERAL

71. Blaisdell, Harold F. **The Philosophical Fisherman.** Boston, Houghton Mifflin, 1969. 384p. $6.95. LC 70-82949. ISBN 0-395-07420-7.

In a thoughtful approach to the art and science of fishing, the philosophical fisherman asks why fish behave as they do and why anglers are successful or unsuccessful in their attempts to catch their finny quarry. While skill in casting or bait presentation is important, more vital is the ability to understand fish, their habits, and the factors that may alter those habits. Very pleasant reading.

72. Gerlach, Rex. **Fly Fishing the Lakes.** New York, Winchester, 1972. 163p. illus. bibliog. index. $6.95. LC 72-79358. ISBN 0-87691-075-4.

Fly fishing is usually connected to stream fishing in the minds of anglers, but Gerlach has learned the secrets of successful fly fishing in lakes. In this book he shares these secrets and explains differences in the two habitats. As streams become more crowded and more polluted, lakes will have to absorb the pressure from the growing ranks of fishermen. Those who want to get ahead of the rush to the lakes and away from the rush on the streams can achieve a substantial measure of self-reeducation with the help of this volume.

73. Gingrich, Arnold. **The Well-Tempered Angler.** New York, Knopf, 1966. 331p. index. $6.95. LC 65-18755. ISBN 0-394-45141-4.

Gingrich, editor and publisher of *Esquire* magazine, first considered *The Fishing Life* as the title for this volume; that, perhaps, sums up the contents very well. The series of essays and personal narratives of fishing experiences over a span of more than 50 years explain a sportsman's feelings about fish and fishing. Fishing is much more than just catching fish–it is seeing the beauty of a brown trout or a grayling, thrilling to the tug and leap of a marlin, or enjoying the companionship of others who love the sport. The author has fished with such literary lights as John Dos Passos and Ernest Hemingway, and with many of those who are better known as fishermen than as writers. Along with the personal experiences on streams and at sea are many pieces of information about fishing that can be pulled out and applied by the reader. Perhaps, too, the reading will help one to mature and grow wiser in the angling art.

74. Harbour, Dave. **Super Freshwater Fishing Systems**. Harrisburg, Pa., Stackpole, 1971. 159p. illus. $7.95. LC 76-140748. ISBN 0-8117-1712-7.

Tactics for catching nearly all major fresh-water game fish and pan fish are described. Harbour also discusses specific brand names of equipment and lures that he has found most effective, which should bring joy to the hearts of the manufacturers of the favored products. In spite of superior products, superior skills, and superior knowledge, catching still is not a guaranteed, sure-fire business that cannot miss. If it were, there would soon be few fish left in our waters and no fun at all. Heavily illustrated, the book is written more for the experienced fisherman than the beginner, and some parts and terms may be difficult for the latter to understand.

75. Janes, Edward C., ed. **Fishing with Ray Bergman**. New York, Knopf, 1970. 328p. $8.95. LC 74-98641. ISBN 0-394-42504-9.

Monthly columns on fishing by the late Ray Bergman are herein compiled, edited, and arranged by Janes to provide a well-organized compendium of instruction in the fine art of fishing. Although trout were Bergman's first and greatest love, other species were sought and were included in his writings—panfish, bass, pike, muskies, and others. His love of woods and waters is obvious in his writing; one writes best about that which he loves most.

76. Lyons, Nick. **The Seasonable Angler**. New York, Funk & Wagnalls, 1970. 177p. $5.95. LC 71-95459.

In this somewhat autobiographical work, Lyons writes of himself as the seasonable angler. Philosophical and slightly mad, as are all avid anglers, he explains each season of the year and its effect on fish and fishermen, and he tells of his own experiences, beginning as a youth fishing with worms, and ending as a fly fisherman, perhaps even a purist. The images evoked by excellent and delicate writing make this book a delight to read. Fishing is not only an active pursuit, but also a state of mind.

77. Morrison, Morie. **Fresh-Water Fishing Illustrated**. Menlo Park, Calif., Lane Books, 1965. 80p. illus. $1.95. LC 65-13364. ISBN 0-376-06221-5.

This concise guide on "how to catch fish in the West" is one of the well-known Sunset books and presents the game fish, lures, and fishing methods used most commonly in the western part of the 48 contiguous states, beginning with the Rocky Mountain area. Illustrations are cartoon-type line drawings. Seasons, limits, and license fees (subject to change) are given. As a brief, low-priced introduction or guide for beginner or tourist, it is adequate; but those seeking greater depth of study or more detailed instruction will want to look elsewhere.

78. Power, John, and Jeremy Brown. **The Fisherman's Handbook: A Complete Guide to Fishing in North America**. New York, Scribner's, 1972. 192p. illus. index. $7.95. LC 70-38529. SBN 684-12845-4.

So many books are available to provide instructions on how to fish and where to fish that reviews eventually begin to sound like extra verses to the same song; yet each volume provides another viewpoint, another set of experiences, or some new information that may be useful to anglers fishing strange waters or learning to cope with new lures, tackle, or unusual conditions. The present work is, in many ways, a repeat of things said before by numerous writers, although new views are recognized. The most useful feature is a listing of the various species of fish of the North American continent north of Mexico, frequency (abundant or present) in each state or province, average size, record sizes, description of each species, and brief angling tips. The distinction between "abundant" and "present" is not clear, and further inquiry of state or provincial game and fish departments would be advisable. An additional listing is provided by state, giving the addresses of those departments and a brief statement on the major fishing waters within the state and the species to be caught.

79. Waterman, Charles F. **The Fisherman's World**. New York, Random House, 1972. 250p. illus. bibliog. index. $15.00. LC 71-176122. ISBN 0-394-41099-8.

All types of fishing in and on the edge of the mainland United States are discussed, but the form of presentation is the most unique feature. Water runs downhill, so the author begins his narrative in the high country where rivers and rivulets begin, then follows the water down to the plains, the valleys, through lakes to the larger rivers, and eventually to the sea. At each stage the type of fishing varies–trout in the high country, bass in the plains areas, catfish, perch, and other species along the way, and finally the coastal salt-water fish. Ecology and habitat of each step are examined to better acquaint the angler with the underwater world of the fish, its food requirements, natural shelters, and habits. Most illustrations are in color.

BASS

80. Bergman, Ray. **Fresh-Water Bass**. Illus. by Fred Hildebrandt. New York, Knopf, 1969. 436p. illus. index. $8.95. ISBN 0-394-40924-8.

Bergman's first love is trout, a fact which he admits, but bass run a close second. First published in 1942, the book is now in its tenth printing—a testimonial to the value and popularity of the subject, the author, and the book. Bass are spread over most of the nation and can thrive in a wide range of waters. Bergman fished for large mouth and small mouth but had less experience with white bass, which have not become so widespread. Bait fishing, plugging, or casting flies all have their moments, and technical information abounds in the work. Bergman is a teacher par excellence; his textbook is an American classic.

81. Circle, Homer. **The Art of Plug Fishing**. Harrisburg, Pa., Stackpole, 1965. 224p. illus. $6.95. LC 65-21621. ISBN 0-8117-0165-4.

Sports Afield's Special Features Editor, Homer Circle, has divided his book into five parts, beginning with "Being an Artful Fisherman," wherein he asks and answers the question most commonly asked by those outside the fraternity, "Why go fishing?" He then goes on to discuss the times for fishing, how to catch bass, and how to clean, cook, and garnish it after it is home. Section two, on tackle, delves into such matters as why some plugs are successful and others are not, why some colors attract fish, and how to tie the proper knots to attach plugs, lines, swivels, and other paraphernalia to the reel at home base. Plugging techniques, or how to make them work for you to the best advantage; facts about fish (mostly bass, trout, and pike); and plug fishing tricks of the experts round out the last three sections. Just as there are devotees of fly fishing and, more particularly, dry fly fishing, so also must those who swear by the plug have their day and their say. It is said very well, too.

82. Dalrymple, Byron. **Modern Book of the Black Bass**. New York, Winchester, 1972. 256p. illus. index. $6.95. LC 79-188592. ISBN 0-87691-066-5.

The bass have had it! Anglers have been practicing and learning for years, but now scientists have gotten into the act to remove the lid from fishy secrets, and Dalrymple has turned the results loose. Research shows that bass can see colors and shades of colors; they have very definite likes and dislikes in forms of shelters; they move and eat according to definite, definable factors. The problem remaining is to determine which factor is affecting them at the moment the bait is cast. Even with all the information available, the day of guaranteed catches is not yet here, and hopefully never will arrive. The fun and challenge would be gone.

TROUT & SALMON

83. Bates, Joseph D., Jr. **Atlantic Salmon Flies and Fishing**. Harrisburg, Pa., Stackpole, 1970. 362p. illus. (color plates). index. $14.95. LC 76-123401. ISBN 0-8117-0180-8.

Each fisherman has his favorite quarry, and each species of fish his following. The salmon, and more specifically, the Atlantic salmon, is no different, being considered by his devotees as the greatest game fish alive. Each writer advances his experiences and shares the results of many years of study along streams and study of the writings of fellow piscatorial students. Bates shares his knowledge of the methods used in salmon fishing, the many wet and dry flies and streamers. Part two of this work, comprising the last seven chapters, discusses fly patterns in considerable depth. The combination of these chapters and the colored plates scattered throughout should enable fly tiers to develop their own collections against the time the fish run again.

84. Bergman, Ray. **Trout**. 2nd rev. ed. New York, Knopf, 1971. 482p. illus. index. $12.50. LC 51-11995. ISBN 0-394-41024-6.

The late Ray Bergman has been referred to as the American answer to Izaak Walton, and *Trout*, first published in 1938, is the classic and standard work on flies and trout fishing. Bergman, Angling Editor of *Outdoor Life* for 26 years, wrote a monthly column for fishermen. This book puts together a lifetime of thought and expertise for a thorough study of fishing for trout with wet and dry flies, nymphs, and spinning equipment. There are 20 beautifully colored plates of flies, with a description of each one for the tier, plus basic instruction on the tying art.

85. Bigelow, Ogden. **Mulberry Trout; or, The Delights of Dry Fly Fishing: A Collection of Fishing Stories**. Rutland, Vt., Tuttle, 1969. 213p. illus. $5.00. LC 69-16177. SBN 8048-0194-0.

Mulberry Trout is a curious title designed for the sole purpose of arousing curiosity. A random collection of stories about Banker Bigelow's fishing exploits, written with great humor, some poetry that would make an English professor shudder, and cartoons by Lee Bart, result in a highly amusing evening's pastime. The Banker's first grandson was even named (temporarily) Steelhead, in honor of his grandfather's love for fishing. One feels that the author enjoyed the writing almost as much as he enjoyed the fishing. There is no attempt to be pedantic or to present his experiences or skills as the last word in how to fish, but rather the thought is conveyed that it has all been a ball and that others will enjoy sharing the fun. These are stories that cry out for a group of fishermen gathered around a hot, potbellied stove on a gloomy day.

86. Brooks, Joe. **Trout Fishing**. New York, Harper & Row, 1972. 302p. illus. index. (An Outdoor Life Book). $8.95. LC 70-178838. ISBN 0-06-010532-1.

The author, Joe Brooks, has established his qualification to write on trout fishing by becoming internationally known as a fisherman, writer, and fishing editor of *Outdoor Life* magazine. Brooks offers new information and new approaches to old information in his book, which is a narrative of his personal experiences with trout fishing in many nations. He provides insights into the similarities of universally used flies, as well as into models used only in certain localities. His detailed chapter on casting techniques is excellent, with noteworthy line drawings. That chapter alone is worth the price of the book for the beginner and is an excellent review for the expert. The color photographs are unusual and add to this well-written book.

87. Corodimas, Peter, ed. **In Trout Country**. Boston, Little, Brown, 1971. 300p. illus. $8.95. LC 79-143713. ISBN 0-316-15743-0.

Essays and short stories compiled into an anthology deal with the pursuit and capture of trout. There are writings of Jesse Hill Ford, Robert Traver, Philip Wylie, Ernest Hemingway, Edward Week, and many others. Among the fishing fraternity, trout are idealized as the most perfect fish, the most worthy antagonist; the successful trout angler is usually felt to be a cut above his fellow men, even those who catch salt-water monsters.

88. Dick, Lenox. **The Art and Science of Fly Fishing**. Rev. ed. New York, Winchester, 1972. 169p. illus. index. $6.95. LC 70-163777. ISBN 0-87691-053-3.

"The *art* of fly-fishing is the skill and grace with which the angler casts his fly. The *science* of fly-fishing uses the knowledge of where fish are, how they feed, and how properly to present a fly" (Introduction). Excellent instructions on choosing and using fly fishing tackle make good reading. While it is easy to learn about handling a fly rod from a book, the actual practice is something else. Dick leads the reader through the practice of basic skills, then follows it up with actual fishing situations on a stream. Trout, steelhead, and salmon are the targets in the Pacific Northwest.

89. Gordon, Theodore, and a company of Anglers. **American Trout Fishing**. Ed. by Arnold Gingrich. New York, Knopf, 1972. 247p. $6.95. LC 65-22952. ISBN 0-394-41625-2.

Dedicated to the memory of Theodore Gordon, 1854-1915, these articles have been collected to preserve his memory and to advance the cause and knowledge of fly fishing for trout. The lead article is by Gordon, the others by followers and admirers known as The Theodore Gordon Flyfishers, who published this volume in 1965 under a different title in a limited edition. All but one of the articles concern fishing in the northeastern corner of the United States, an area considered by some to be the Mecca of American trout angling. Each piece of writing is different, following no scheme or design; some are informative, some humorous, and others are narratives of fishing experiences.

90. Hidy, V. S. **The Pleasures of Fly Fishing**. New York, Winchester, 1972. 127p. illus. bibliog. $10.00. LC 77-159428. ISBN 0-87691-039-8.

Photography and philosophy! Hidy has made many photos, both color and black and white, of fishermen's dream streams and lakes, then set them off with philosophic quotations from a great many sources. The combination is beautiful, peaceful, soothing, yet exciting. All pictures appear to have been made in the western United States, where skies are still free from heavy pollution and colors are brilliant. Although camera data for each shot are not included, a brief note of instruction for the shutterbug is added at the end.

91. McDonald, John. **Quill Gordon**. New York, Knopf, 1972. 196p. illus. index. $10.95. LC 72-2253. ISBN 0-394-46989-5.

The Quill Gordon is the name of a trout fly named for Theodore Gordon, one of the most famous names in American fly fishing history; this book is, of course, about fly fishing and its history and development. Erudite, but not boring, the history is recounted with thorough documentation. There are seven colored plates of old and new trout and salmon flies. Many personal experiences are recalled to introduce the study of a fly, a stream, or of insects that are the basis of most flies. An excellent study is made of the famous Green Drake, or mayfly, as it exists in the

British Isles and in this country. There are twelve trout fly patterns described from the 1450 edition of *Treatise of Fishing with an Angle* using the original fifteenth century language, followed by the modern description. Historical perspective is the theme throughout, in contrast to the how-to books.

92. Marinaro, Vincent C. **A Modern Dry-Fly Code**. New ed. New York, Crown, 1970. 269p. illus. $10.00; $50.00 limited edition. LC 76-120292.

Spending much time in the study of dry-fly imitations of real insects, Marinaro has developed artificial insects such as the grasshopper and the Japanese beetle because he believes, from observation and experience, that terrestrial artificials are more effective than aquatic artificials. That is, there are times when fish prefer and feed on land-based insects in preference to those that hatch and/or live in water. It was ten years after the first edition of this work that it began to receive the recognition it deserved. It is now a classic, according to the aficionados, and first editions have sold for over $100.

93. Miller, Alfred W. **Fishless Days, Angling Nights**. By Sparse Grey Hackle (pseud.). New York, Crown, 1971. 224p. photos. $7.50. LC 76-163083.

Sparse Grey Hackle is really expert trout fisherman A. W. Miller, or vice versa. His contributions over the past three decades have been primarily for the "Angler's Club Bulletin," but he has also written for sports magazines. His current offering is an anthology of previous works, reminiscences, little vignettes, and just stories. In keeping with the present national mood, there is much nostalgia for days past, but the light approach prevails. Pleasant and entertaining reading without the hard sell of some publications, which insist that the reader do things a certain way.

94. Orvis, Charles F., and A. Nelson Cheney, comp. **Fishing with the Fly**. New York, Houghton Mifflin, 1886; Rutland, Vt., Tuttle, 1968. 328p. colored plates. $8.25. LC 67-25012. ISBN 0-8048-0181-9.

Orvis was a well-known maker of fine fishing tackle and tier of flies, and the firm that he founded is still in existence. With Cheney, he collected a number of articles about all kinds of fly fishing—trout, salmon, bass, and grayling, for the most part. The language of that period may at times seem quaint to the present-day reader, but there is no misunderstanding its meaning. All the contributors were fond of fishing the fly, and one, L. A. Beardslee, was greatly affronted when he failed to interest trout and salmon in Alaska without using bait. Fifteen colored plates of salmon, trout, and bass flies as made by Orvis are all indexed for quick reference. With each plate is a collection of brief quotations from earlier writers such as Sir Walter Scott, Izaak Walton, Washington Irving, Henry Thoreau, Daniel Webster, and others.

95. Ritz, Charles. **A Fly Fisher's Life**. New American ed. Trans. by Humphrey Hare. New York, Winchester, 1969. 230p. illus. $12.50. LC 60-7400. SBN 87476-0110.

Fly fishing, primarily for trout and salmon, has been the author's pleasure and relaxation throughout his life. His writing includes experiences on the streams and lakes of Europe and North America, with detailed analysis of fly casting techniques. A thorough study of the use of arm muscles helps to understand the processes of fly casting under varying conditions. Line drawings illustrate casting movements. Fly patterns of the author's favorites are included for tiers.

96. Scholes, David. **Trout Quest**. Melbourne, Australia, Lansdowne; distr. New Rochelle, N.Y., Sportshelf, 1969. 215p. line drawings. $13.50. LC 75-467133. ISBN 0-392-00049-0.

According to the dust jacket, Australia has some of the best trout fishing in the world, but probably few Americans know about it. In fact, few know much about Australia at all. Scholes' tales of fishing "down under" are entertaining and each one has a point. The book is divided into three main parts: the first, "Essence of Things," is on tackle and techniques; the second, called "General Tactics," is a series of stories of fishing in varying waters, differing seasons, and with a variety of lures; the third, "Thoughts and Reflections," is again a series of experiences but with a more philosophical twist. Overall, the book is charming, informative, and good reading.

97. Schwiebert, Ernest. **Remembrances of Rivers Past**. New York, Macmillan, 1972. 224p. $5.95. LC 71-167929.

We all have great moments in our lives, moments that remain bright in our thoughts for many years or for life. Schwiebert shares some of his best memories as a fly fisherman, telling of his experiences on the rivers in Michigan, Colorado, Wyoming, New York, and Pennsylvania. He first began fly fishing in the rivers of Michigan, seeking trout, and has since fished many other waters, including some in the South American Andes and the Asian Himalayas. From his experience he gives helpful information on particular streams and the most successful methods that he has used. All is not roses at all times, however, and he does not hesitate to tell of his failures.

98. Ure, James. **Bait for Trout: Being the Confessions of an Unorthodox Angler**. Chicago, Regnery, 1973. 170p. illus. $5.95. LC 72-11189.

There are six main species of trout; the author describes each one in its natural habitat, gives helpful tips on recognizing favorable water conditions, and tells what type of bait is best. Text is replete with photographs and line drawings of trout, bait, and bait fishing techniques. Included is a directory of equipment manufacturers and suppliers of bait; there are also some of Ure's favorite trout recipes and fish stories. While bait is quite practical, the very idea is likely to put some dry-fly purists into orbit.

99. Wright, Leonard M., Jr. **The Thinking Man's Guide to Trout Angling: An Unorthodox Method of Fishing the Dry Fly as a Living Insect**. New York, Dutton, 1972. 192p. $6.95. LC 70-190374.

Wright believes that there are two types of fly fishermen: the imitationists, who strive to tie flies that are as similar to living insects as possible; and the presentationists, who are most concerned with properly casting and laying the fly on the water in the manner of the real insect. He, on the other hand, is a behaviorist, contending that the fly must behave like the insect in its movements while within the field of vision of the fish. This, of course, is a form of presentation and the fly should conform in appearance to the natural food. Behaviorism is concerned with matching the hatch by studying water and air temperatures and any other factors that affect the insects in each locality. According to the author, a fish that sees correct behavior is more likely to take the lure, even if it is a poor imitation, than it is to take the perfect imitation when it doesn't act right. Manipulation, then, is more important than imitation or presentation.

WALLEYE

100. Fellegy, Joe. **Walleyes and Walleye Fishing**. Minneapolis, Dillon Press, 1973. 210p. illus. maps. $6.95. LC 72-89440. ISBN 0-87518-54-X.

As with trout, bass, or any other specie, walleyes require an approach and technique suitable to their habits and habitats. Instructions in these techniques, choice of tackle and baits are provided by the author, an experienced fishing guide. He includes a guide to the distribution of walleyes, whose range is changing as they are planted into waters far from their original homes. The end result of fishing is the table, so recipes are given to help gain the most from the final enjoyment of angling. Numerous articles can be located on the walleye, but this may be the only book in captivity devoted completely to this one fish.

Fly Tying

101. Bates, Joseph D., Jr. **Streamer Fly Tying and Fishing**. Harrisburg, Pa., Stackpole, 1966. 368p. illus. (part col.). index. $7.95. LC 66-12782. ISBN 0-8117-1692-9.

Fly tying and streamer tying is an art form just as much as sculpture or painting even though it may not be recognized as such by the world of fine arts. It requires talent, a sharp eye, and skill to do a first class job. It is also one of the useful arts, providing sport and food to the user. Bates shows 119 patterns of streamers and bucktails in full color on eight plates and gives instructions for tying, or dressing, over 300 patterns for both salt- and fresh-water fishing. In addition, he tells of his personal experiences and knowledge acquired in the proper and artful use of these lures to attract and fool fish. Each type of lure, dry fly, plug, worm, or streamer must be handled in the right way if it is to simulate food, a territorial intruder, or something else to the fish and thereby gain a strike. With the tying data is included a history of each pattern.

102. Flick, Art, ed. **Art Flick's Master Fly-Tying Guide**. New York, Crown, 1972. 207p. illus. index. $10.00. LC 72-85693. ISBN 0-517-50023-X.

There are fly tiers who fish, those who don't, and fishermen who tie flies and others that don't. Among those fly tiers of either variety, Art Flick is a recognized master of the art. He has drawn contributions from other experts to present an overall picture of modern fly tying methods, materials, and patterns. Color, which is essential to convey the feeling of many flies, especially the more exotic, has been well used here. The fly fisherman who learns to tie his own lures will discover that the thrills are greater when he has tied the fly that fools a wily old lunker.

103. Leiser, Eric. **Fly Tying Materials**. New York, Crown, 1973. 224p. illus. $7.50. LC 72-96650.

As a dealer in fly tying materials and equipment, the author should be well qualified to speak on the subject. He gives much information that cannot be easily found elsewhere, such as how to dye feathers and fur, import regulations controlling animal products, how to raise your own birds, how to preserve the skins, and how to use synthetic materials. Raising birds for their feathers might save time and money for the craftsman, but again it might not, since the birds require space, time, feed, and a fair amount of equipment. City residents may find that ordinances prohibit such activities within residential zones so a check with City Hall should be made first. Information for the most part is quite useful.

104. Schwiebert, Ernest. **Nymphs: A Complete Guide to Naturals and Imitations**. New York, Winchester, 1973. 370p. illus. bibliog. index. $9.95. LC 73-188596. ISBN 0-87691-074-6.

Author of *Matching the Hatch* (Macmillan, 1962) and *Remembrances of Rivers Past* (Macmillan, 1972), Schwiebert now matches the pre-hatch. Nymphs are the early stages of insects before they metamorphose and become adults, and in that pre-adult stage are delicacies for fish. The fisherman, then, following the writer's precepts learns some entomology, learns to tie flies that simulate the nymphs of various species such as the caddis, stone, and mayflies, then proceeds to fish them. Imitation nymphs have been in use for a long time, but until now there has not been a satisfactory study presented to relate them to fishing. This fills a serious gap in piscatorial literature.

Chapter 5

FIREARMS

Modern Firearms

MISCELLANEOUS

105. Ackley, Parker O. **Home Gun Care and Repair**. Harrisburg, Pa., Stackpole, 1969. 191p. illus. index. $5.95. LC 69-16147. ISBN 0-8117-0809-8.

P. O. Ackley, who is one of the best-known authorities in the field of custom gunsmithing today, presents a quick reference book for the many repairs and improvement projects that can be undertaken by the average gun owner. The author explains, in very clear, precise, non-technical terms, specific repair techniques that the home craftsman can carry out safely on his own guns with a reasonable investment in tools and equipment. Most people probably already have a major portion of the tools on hand for other jobs on their autos or their homes. Ackley stresses the importance of a thorough knowledge of the mechanics of guns before making the repairs. Details are given on care and repair of rifles, shotguns, and handguns. Illustrations are limited but the text is sufficiently descriptive to serve without additional pictures.

106. **Guns Illustrated, 1972: The Journal for Gun Buffs**. Ed. by Joseph J. Schroeder, Jr., and editors of Gun Digest. Deluxe 4th ed. Chicago, Follett, 1971. 288p. illus. index. $3.95pa. LC 79-11342. SBN 695-80224-0.

Gun Digest set out to cover thoroughly the field of firearms currently available in this country for sporting use and for collecting, and has succeeded admirably. Quality has obviously been an important consideration, because the cheap "Saturday night specials" are conspicuous by their absence. This fourth annual edition contains a wealth of information in an easy-to-use format. Besides the basic illustrated information on guns, both domestic and imported, there are extensive articles for shooters and collectors, ranging from firearms legislation through loading to specialized items of both current and historical interest. One item of particular interest is a two-page list of instructions of do's, don't's, and how-to's for survival in either forests or deserts under all conditions. A guide to the arms trade contains over 1,200 names and addresses of firms supplying products and/or services to shooters, gunsmiths, and dealers. Copiously illustrated, well indexed, a bargain for the price.

107. Kuhlhoff, Pete. **Kuhlhoff on Guns**. New York, Winchester, 1970. 180p. illus. index. $5.95. LC 70-99751. ISBN 0-87691-009-6.

Kuhlhoff has long been recognized as an authority on guns and, his columns and articles have appeared in many sporting journals. This volume is a general survey of shooting with all long guns–rifles and shotguns of all calibers and gauges, for all purposes from plinking to hunting. Although handguns are included, shoulder arms are given most attention. Handloading and gun collecting are discussed in two chapters. In a general, chatty survey of the wide field of gunning, Kuhlhoff has done an excellent job.

108. Lind, Ernie. **The Complete Book of Trick and Fancy Shooting**. New York, Winchester, 1972. 159p. illus. $5.95. LC 79-159431. ISBN 0-87691-045-2.

Although the day of the exhibition shooter seems to be pretty well gone, there are still a few experts around who might revive interest in the art. Lind, who has been demonstrating his skill for over 30 years, tells how all the trick and fancy shooting is done. Learning the basic steps in hitting the targets–small objects tossed in the air–is only a small step. Constant practice is the major key, with the author recommending a thousand or more practice shots each week until real proficiency is attained.

Description of the more spectacular events in an exhibition shoot is excellent, and there is an explanation of how to detect fakery, frequently used in carnivals.

109. Moreton, Dave, ed. **Gun Talk**. New York, Winchester, 1973. 250p. illus. $7.95. LC 72-96091. ISBN 0-87691-105-X.

A collection of 18 articles covering every major phase of shooting from the pens of America's best-known shooting writers, this is an excellent compact reference book for hunters and targeteers. Askins, Barrett, Kuhlhoff, O'Connor, and others have each contributed a chapter on that aspect of shooting that each knows best. The use of black powder for shooting antiques or replicas has enjoyed a comeback in the last few years, and Hal Swiggett talks about its use and terminology. Ken Waters, on the other hand, is interested in shooting the old Winchesters and Marlins, the kind usually found in collections or hanging on the wall, retired because their owners think that they are no longer safe. When the gun is in good condition, and loads are built that the old steel can handle safely, there is still a lot of pleasure and use in the old timers. These chapters, and many others on modern guns, make a very useful manual for the hunter/plinker/target shooter.

110. Petzal, David E., ed. **The Experts' Book of the Shooting Sports**. Cord Communications: Simon & Schuster, 1972. 320p. illus. index. $9.95. LC 72-83904. ISBN 0-671-21328-8.

As the title indicates, this book is a complete survey of all phases of shooting sports; articles are written by experts who are well-known for their writings as well as for their abilities in shooting and hunting. The book is divided into sections. The section on rifle shooting covers target and benchrest shooting and four types of hunting; the handgun section deals with target shooting and hunting; and the shotgun segment treats trapshooting, skeet shooting, and three distinct hunting situations. The last section in this volume is devoted to the discussion of shooting optics, custom guns, and the care, cleaning, and repair of firearms. This is not a how-to book in the usual sense, but it does define the various aspects of the shooting game.

111. **E. C. Prudhomme, Master Gun Engraver**. Shreveport, La., R. W. Norton Art Gallery, 1973. 32p. illus. $3.00. LC 73-78704. ISBN 0-913060-01-1.

The engravings of Edward Clark Prudhomme were exhibited at the Norton Gallery from April 1 to May 13, 1973. Works displayed were done from 1946 to 1973, and this publication is a descriptive, illustrated catalog. Most photos are close-ups to better show the fine detail of the engraver's work. In addition to engraving, there are many fine examples of gold, silver, and platinum inlays, usually of deer, bear, mountain sheep, elk, and other game animals and birds. Engraved firearms shown are rifles, pistols, revolvers, and shotguns of both foreign and domestic manufacture. Each illustration has a description of the arm, including serial number, and a description of the work of the engraver. John Amber, editor of *Gun Digest*, wrote a brief biography of Prudhomme as an introduction to the catalog. Although this is primarily an art book illustrating the art form of engraving, it is also highly desirable for gun buffs.

112. **Shooter's Bible**. 1973 ed. Ed. by John Olson. Chicago, Follett, 1973. illus. index. $4.95pa. LC 63-6220. ISBN 0-695-80362-X.

Like preceding annual issues, this, the edition of the 64th year, is actually a catalog of firearms and accessories sold by Stoeger Arms Corporation. Most American and many foreign arms are listed, illustrated, and priced along with ammunition, loading components, hunting clothing, telescopes, and shooting glasses. CO_2 guns and pellets, popular for indoor targetry, have been carried for many years. The ballistic tables included in every edition are important to all shooters. Nearly everything of quality in the sporting firearms field is shown if available in this country; conversely, cheap, low-grade weapons, both domestic and foreign, have always been excluded. Scattered throughout the catalog are articles on shooting and hunting by well-known writers in the shooting fraternity. Backfiles of *Shooter's Bible* are maintained by many gunsmiths and sporting goods firms for information on older products that can rarely be found elsewhere. Early editions, when available, frequently command high prices from collectors.

113. **Shooter's Bible Gun Traders Guide**. By Paul Wahl. 5th rev. ed. South Hackensack, N.J., Stoeger Arms Corp., 1968. 220p. illus. $3.95pa. LC 68-59113.

This is the latest edition of a gun trader's guide to pricing of most of the rifles, shotguns, and handguns, both American and foreign, that are likely to be encountered during the course of business. To avoid guesswork and the financial loss that might result from guessing, a guide such as this, or Chapel's handbook (No. 145) is quite useful to traders and collectors. Pricing, however, can vary widely from year to year and from one part of the country to another. Prices of antique guns, as well as of modern used guns, are based almost exclusively on supply and demand. Seasonal variations in prices must be contended with, too, especially in good used hunting arms.

114. **Shooter's Bible Small Arms Lexicon and Concise Encyclopedia**. By Chester Mueller and John Olson. South Hackensack, N.J., Shooter's Bible; distr. Chicago, Follett, 1968. 390p. illus. $14.95. LC 67-30798.

Most trades and professions have a language or jargon of terms used within the trade to simplify communication, each word or phrase having a meaning clearly understood by all practitioners. Examples of these specialized "languages" are readily noted in dictionaries of medicine, philosophy, psychology, education, and others. In many instances, words will be common to more than one profession, but the meanings attached will differ widely. *The Small Arms Lexicon and Concise Encyclopedia*, a guide to the language of the firearms trade, gives words and phrases common to that trade throughout five centuries, with many photos and drawings to clarify definitions. Many terms are no longer used except in historical research and writing, and others have become common expressions in everyday life, with little or no realization of their origins. "Flash in the pan," "dud," "going off half-cocked," and "trigger-happy" are familiar expressions that originated in the firearms trade. In addition to the lexicon of terms, this volume contains 25 tables on ballistics, woods for gunstocks, metals, mathematical conversion tables, trade directories, and others.

115. Smith, W. H. B. **Small Arms of the World: A Basic Manual of Military Small Arms.** 9th ed., rev. by Joseph E. Smith. Harrisburg, Pa., Stackpole, 1969. 768p. illus. index. $17.95. LC 72-90881. ISBN 0-8117-1565-5.

The late W. H. B. Smith's work on small arms has long been a standard reference work on the subject; updating and revising has been carried on by his brother. The coverage of small arms includes handguns, shoulder weapons, machine guns, flare guns, etc., but excludes those weapons usually referred to as "cannon," however small. The first part of the book discusses the history and development of military weapons, while the second part consists of detailed descriptions of the guns themselves. Almost all nations are included—42 to be exact—even though some of the smaller ones use guns imported from another country and have none that might be called their own. Countries without a separate listing are usually mentioned somewhere in the text. Nations formed after publication of a given edition, of course, will not be listed until the subsequent edition.

Information provided includes makes, models, types, calibers, field stripping instructions, loading and firing procedures for each one, with drawings to explain the mechanical operation of some, gives the reader pretty complete information. In view of the constantly changing technology, holders of older editions will certainly need the updating of this new one.

116. Steindler, Robert A. **The Firearms Dictionary**. Harrisburg, Pa., Stackpole, 1970. 288p. illus. index. $7.95. LC 75-107957. SBN 8117-0614-1.

Steindler, editor of *Shooting Times* magazine, a frequent contributor to other sporting publications, and author of other books on firearms, has recognized the need for both a presentation and a standardization of terms in the firearms field. This book is quite similar in content to the *Shooter's Bible Small Arms Lexicon and Concise Encyclopedia* (entry 114), but a comparison of the two shows that there is, at times, a variation in definitions for the same term; variation in the wording used to define terms, with one or the other publication being more expansive; variation in the depth of coverage or extent of explanation for varying uses of a term. Both publications are excellent; further comparison demonstrates clearly that neither book replaces nor makes useless the other, since each lists much that cannot be found in the other. Illustrations in the *Firearms Dictionary* are line drawings and photographs to clarify a definition. "See" and "see also" cross references are used frequently and well. Except for a few photographs that are somewhat dark, the book is of excellent quality in printing and binding.

117. Wallack, L. R. **The Anatomy of Firearms: A Clear, Comprehensive Guide to All Types of Guns, Ammunition and Ballistics, plus Do-It-Yourself Repairs and Adjustments**. Intro. by Larry Koller. New York, Maco Pub. (Simon & Schuster), 1965. 320p. photos. $6.95. LC 65-27690.

In the first section of the book, the author presents the mechanical operations of the six types of sporting firearms. The rest of the book is devoted to the components of the gun: stocks, sights, barrels and receivers, ammunition. There are four chapters covering elementary ballistics, in proper sequence, from the firing pin fall to the bullet striking the target; however, none of the mathematics of ballistics is included. The explanation is one of the clearest available outside of technical journals. Numerous drawings and photographs accompany the text, although some are quite dark. The verbal illustrations are very well done and more than offset the pictorial failings. Wallack, a gunsmith, lists some of the jobs that the home craftsman can do to improve his own arms and warns against attempting others that require special skill and equipment.

RIFLES

118. Lachuk, John, and others. **Wonderful World of the .22**. Los Angeles, Petersen Pub. Co., 1972. 192p. illus. $2.95pa. LC 72-83658.

.22 caliber rifles and pistols have been popular guns for over a hundred years, and that popularity has not diminished. According to the author, approximately four *billion* .22 cartridges are fired each year, down from five billion before the 1968 Gun Control Act was put into effect to make the purchase of guns and ammunition more difficult for the honest citizen. Extensive use of the .22 results from the relatively low cost of guns and ammunition, making it possible for almost anyone to enjoy an afternoon or weekend "plinking" at tin cans, spoiled fruit, clay balls, or paper targets. Glass bottles are taboo on environmental grounds, and cans and paper should not be left lying around after shooting. Some shoot to relieve tension and enjoy the outdoors while others are serious, competitive target buffs. Articles on every facet of .22's from choice and purchase through survival shooting to self-defense provide a complete picture of small-bore arms. Most shooters probably do not know that there are .22 shot shells, but data on patterns and penetration are included. Test results on a number of guns, both rifles and pistols, show qualities, capabilities, and features. A catalog of optics lists 49 telescopic sights used on .22's, sold by 16 manufacturers at prices ranging from $8.25 up to $45.00. The listing of firearms shows 95 rifles priced from $25.00 to $195.00 for sporting models, and on up to $414.00 for a super-fine target model, and 88 handguns from $37.95 to $350.00. These are all quality arms, no junk, so the popularity is proven. Manufacturers do not put out such a wide choice of products without good reason.

119. O'Connor, Jack. **The Big-Game Rifle**. New York, Knopf, 1952. 370p. illus. index. $10.00. LC 51-11987. ISBN 0-394-41684-8.

O'Connor dislikes the term "authority" when it is applied to writers (including himself) who publish facts and/or opinions about sporting rifles and their use for certain types of game; nevertheless, most sportsmen who read outdoors magazines or books think of him as an authority on big game rifles. O'Connor has hunted North America, Africa, India, and other parts of the world and speaks from experience about the arms he has used or has observed in use. In the present volume he examines the many aspects of rifle selection and use for hunting—guns, ammunition and its components, and accessories. Factory guns and custom guns have their points as do high velocity bullets and slow velocity/heavy weight bullets. Requirements for soft-skinned game differ from those for the thick-skinned animals because of problems of penetration, and dangerous game needs to be met with greater stopping power than non-dangerous species. His conclusion, after all considerations, is that the man behind the gun is the most important element and that skill resulting from practice cannot be replaced by more powerful or more expensive weapons. For an interesting change in O'Connor's attitude, see *The Hunting Rifle* (next entry).

120. O'Connor, Jack. **The Hunting Rifle**. New York, Winchester, 1970. 314p. illus. index. $8.95. LC 72-99749. ISBN 0-87691-007-X.

Eighteen years after *The Big-Game Rifle* comes *The Hunting Rifle*, which reflects a pronounced change in attitude in many respects but which retains the excellent quality of analysis of guns and their uses. In the first chapter, O'Connor discusses "authorities" and "experts," pointing out that a great many, even though they have actually had very limited experience in hunting, set themselves up, or accept the accolades of others, as experts and make very specific judgments and recommendations on the value of a certain gun for certain game. He admits that he has been guilty of that sin himself, in the past, when he would "divide game into various classes and smugly recommend cartridges for each." Wider experience has shown him that all is not so cut and dried. The present volume is, to a great extent, an update of the earlier work in that it continues the analysis of ballistics, use of rifles under hunting conditions, and comparisons of the many cartridges available to the hunter. Some of those listed were either very new or not yet developed at the time of the earlier writing. Regardless of his own opinion of the appellation, O'Connor is still an authority in the eyes of many riflemen and hunters.

121. O'Connor, Jack. **The Rifle Book**. 2nd rev. ed. New York, Knopf, 1964. 332p. illus. index. $10.00. LC 62-11053. ISBN 0-394-41016-5.

First published in 1949, the present edition includes new developments in sporting rifles and ammunition that have come on the market in the intervening 15 years. This is not a catalog attempting to list all guns, but rather a selective listing, with descriptions and discussions of the capabilities of the arms. Sighting equipment, types of rifle actions, and cartridges are well presented.

SHOTGUNS

122. Arthur, Robert. **The Shotgun Stock: Design, Construction, and Embellishment**. New York, Barnes, 1971. 175p. illus. index. $12.00. LC 73-107107. ISBN 0-498-07621-0.

Making a stock for a shotgun is much like making one for a rifle, yet there are important differences that must be learned if the finished product is to fit the user. The most critical differences are in drop and pitch, which greatly affect the ability of the shooter to hit his target. Shotguns are brought to the shoulder and fired more quickly and, according to some writers, more instinctively than rifles, which are held carefully for aiming. Arthur digs into the matter of drop and pitch, explains its effect, and tells how to make the stock for the individual gunner. Suitable wood, sights and ribs, the use of cheek pieces, cast off or cast on, and special problems are all examined as they relate to stock manufacture. Checkering, carving, or other forms of ornamentation are largely a matter of the taste of the individual and range from the very plain to the very gaudy.

123. Garwood, Gough Thomas. **Gough Thomas's Gun Book: Shotgun Lore for the Sportsman**. New York, Winchester, 1970. 273p. illus. $8.95. LC 77-119880. ISBN 0-87691-020-7.

Most of the shotguns discussed are of European manufacture, hence of little interest to the average American gunner; but the information on recoil, range determination and capabilities, pattern testing, and general shooting problems is useful anywhere. Thomas is Gun Editor of *Shooting Times* in Great Britain and writes in a popular style. Much of this book is a compilation of his magazine articles.

124. Garwood, Gough Thomas. **Gough Thomas's Second Gun Book**. New York, Winchester, 1972. 227p. illus. index. $8.95. LC 78-188601. ISBN 0-87691-064-9.

More about shotguns, this is a follow-up to the preceding entry. As Gun Editor for *Shooting Times*, a British sportsman's journal, Garwood has written about various problems and answered questions submitted by readers. This book is a compilation of many of his articles rearranged by specific subjects. Each article carries the date of its appearance in *Shooting Times*. Although the author is an Englishman, the problems discussed are universal, such as gun care and handling, shot loads, recoil, etc.

125. Hastings, Macdonald. **How to Shoot Straight**. New York, Barnes, 1970. 133p. photos. index. $5.95. LC 68-29862. ISBN 0-498-06940-0.

Hastings emphasizes his technique of instruction, stressing the body form—how to place the feet, hold the head, grip the gun, and use the arms. He also points out the importance of drilling in the proper form until each part of the drill becomes automatic. Form may not be the cause of all the problems of the poor shooter; on the other hand, instruction on form might be the specific needed by some. Because the author decided to present the shooting methods as they are followed in England, instead of americanizing the language, some of the terminology may be perplexing to the average reader. The book is well done and represents the views of one with experience. There have been numerous books written in the past few years on various ways to increase proficiency with firearms, and especially with shotguns. This latest book falls in the same category. The author demonstrates his method and how it works for him; who knows?—it may be a technique that works for others.

126. Knight, Richard Alden. **Mastering the Shotgun**. Illus. by Pody and Harold Bush. New York, Dutton, 1967. 128p. illus. $4.95. LC 66-11551. ISBN 0-525-15422-1.

There are many other manuals on shotguns and shooting, but Knight's book is somewhat different. Much of the material in this manual on the art of handling a shotgun seems to be "old hat"—but it is all explained with a new outlook, both in training methods and, to a certain extent, in terminology. The author tells of his method and how it worked for him; he could have suggested, "Try it, you'll like it." Using an ordinary kitchen broom for practice while thinking of sweeping the target from the air sounds delightful and interesting. Old-timers will object to much that is said, but how can one argue with a man who has mastered the art of shooting the shotgun? Included are special sections on skeet and trap shooting as well as safety rules that should be in every book dealing with weapons.

127. Missildine, Fred, with Nick Karas. **Score Better at Skeet**. New York, Winchester, 1972. 162p. illus. $5.95. LC 70-129248. ISBN 0-87691-004-5; 0-87691-049-5pa.

Author of *Score Better at Trap* (next entry), Missildine uses the same analytical approach in teaching the art of skeet shooting. Skeet, from a Scandinavian word meaning "to shoot," is a relatively young sport. It began in the 1920s and is similar to trap, but different. Both sports are year-round activities using shotguns, and the same type of clay targets. From this point, however, differences increase–rules, layout of the shooting area, and the problems to be mastered. Missildine proceeds station-by-station around the range and teaches the proper way to shoot skeet from each position in order to become a champion.

128. Missildine, Fred, with Nick Karas. **Score Better at Trap**. New York, Winchester, 1971. 157p. illus. $5.95. LC 79-99745. ISBN 0-87691-025-8; 0-87691-005-3pa.

Trap shooting began as a way of providing off-season practice for hunters. It rapidly grew into a competitive sport engaged in year-round both by hunters and by those who never hunt. Both trap and skeet are enjoyed by a great many women. Live birds were used at first, and later glass balls; today the standard target is a clay dish. The target is still referred to as a bird, or as a clay pigeon. Missildine, an instructor at his own school, discusses guns for trap shooting and problems in learning the sport; he also analyzes each step in shooting a round.

129. Montague, Andrew A., with S. V. Beckwith. **Successful Shotgun Shooting**. New York, Winchester, 1971. 169p. illus. $5.95. LC 70-150348. ISBN 0-87691-034-7.

With an anatomical analysis of body stances and movements required in shotgunning, Montague, an international trap champion, teaches his art through step-by-step instruction. For those shooters having problems, whether in trap, skeet, or hunting, self-analysis and self-reeducation are possible, and the formation or reinforcement of safety habits is always desirable.

130. O'Connor, Jack. **The Shotgun Book**. New York, Knopf, 1972. (Reprint of 1965 ed.) 332p. illus. index. $10.00. LC 64-20172. ISBN 0-394-41019-X.

First published in 1965 and now in its fourth printing, O'Connor's treatise on the shotgun has demonstrated its popularity and reliability. The author has hunted all around the world and has written extensively on hunting and firearms. Beginning with the history of scatterguns, the different types and their purposes and styles are explored. To be successful in shooting, the gun must fit the shooter, must pattern correctly, and for best results must have loads designed for the game sought. The choice of autoloader, double, pump, or single shot is largely a matter of personal taste although each one has its advantages and disadvantages. Instruction for properly handling a shotgun is excellent, but is quite similar to that found in many other works on shooting.

HANDGUNS

131. Josserand, Michel H., and Jan A. Stevenson. **Pistols, Revolvers, and Ammunition**. New York, Crown, 1972. 341p. illus. bibliog. index. $7.50. LC 75-147336.

Authors Josserand and Stevenson examine in great detail the step-by-step function of each system used by various manufacturers of pistols and revolvers to achieve loading, revolving, blow-back, firing, or ejection. They state that the book is meant to be an elementary text and is concerned more with the mechanical operations of handguns than with their history, which can be found in abundance in other works. The explanations are clearly written and the illustrations are attractive and helpful. An important aspect of the book is the excellent discussion of U.S. laws. This title is a translation of an earlier French work by the same authors.

132. Nonte, George. **Shooter's Bible Pistol and Revolver Guide**. New rev. 2nd ed. Chicago, Follett, 1970. 215p. illus. $3.95pa. LC 67-21819. SBN 695-80086-8.

Handgunners with questions and problems are quite likely to find the answers in Nonte's collection of currently available weapons or in the accompanying text. Discussions cover history of hand-held guns (usually one-hand versus the two-hand hold for shoulder weapons), maintenance, ammunition, shooting, and most importantly, safety. Nonte begins in the choosing of a handgun to suit the needs and purposes of the sportsman, then follows through with accessories such as holsters, sights, grips, etc., providing instruction and advice for both the beginner and the experienced. There is also something for the muzzle-loading enthusiast and for the air-gun fan who wants to shoot indoors or in a populated area with safety. A bibliography, a glossary, and a directory of suppliers are added at the end.

133. Weston, Paul B. **The Handbook of Handgunning**. New York, Crown, 1968. 138p. illus. index. $4.95. LC 68-20570.

A former New York City policeman, instructor in that city's Police Academy, gunnery specialist, writer, and currently, a professor at

Sacramento State College in California where he coaches shooting in addition to his other teaching duties, Weston presents a guide for self-teaching in the use of handguns. Numerous illustrations and step-by-step detailed instruction in grip, aiming, and the many factors involved in marksmanship are easily understood by the novice. The course of instruction is not easy, since concentration, hard work, and much practice are required to achieve proficiency. Development of the hand and arm muscles, proper grip, sight picture, stance, and practice are the major points, with practice and more practice and constant reevaluation of form the most important of all. Range procedures and safe handling practices are also emphasized, with a self-diagnosis test in the appendix.

HANDLOADING

134. Nonte, George C., Jr. **Modern Handloading**. New York, Winchester, 1972. 410p. illus. $10.00. LC 73-159427. ISBN 0-87691-046-0.

In an excellent survey of the entire handloading business, Nonte goes into the many details and problems encountered by the home craftsman, from the workbench through tools, supplies, and shooting. His historical survey is shorter than that of Sharpe (next entry), but tools and equipment are much more up to date. He also includes shotshell reloading information, which Sharpe did not. Actual loads are not given—these are available in handbooks published by Lyman, Speer, and others, and are updated frequently. A glossary of terms, tables of ballistics, and other charts and tables are quite useful.

135. Sharpe, Philip Burdette. **Complete Guide to Handloading**. 3rd ed., 2nd rev. New York, Funk & Wagnalls, 1953. 727p. illus. index. $10.00. LC 53-2669.

First published in 1937 by the late Philip Sharpe, this treatise has gone through three editions, numerous revisions, and a great many printings. Many handloaders take exception to the loads proposed herein, but this volume is still considered the classic, standard work on the subject. The history of the development of the modern cartridge and its component parts is long and involved, but a knowledge of the history and an awareness of the many factors to be considered in handloading are necessary to the loader for a thorough understanding of all that takes place when he loads and fires his own ammunition; his life may depend on it. There are pressure limits to be aware of, and at some point above that limit even the best of guns may come unglued in the shooter's hands.

Handled with knowledge and reason, handloading is very safe. The latest edition is now 20 years old and does not include many cartridges, loads, or powders currently popular, but the basic material is still valid and important.

Gunsmithing

136. De Haas, Frank. **Bolt Action Rifles**. Chicago, Follett, 1971. 320p. illus. index. $6.95pa. LC 73-163105. ISBN 0-695-80220-8.

This book was desperately needed: it is a careful evaluation of the quality and safety of the bolt actions, especially military actions, that have been used for many years for the construction of sporting arms. Both professional and amateur gunsmiths, but especially amateurs, are concerned with the safety of an action for a cartridge other than the one for which the action was originally manufactured. Professionals, with wider experience, are better able to determine safety factors for themselves, but they still have questions and doubts about some makes and models. Assembly/disassembly instructions, history, dimensions, and miscellaneous other data are given for the actions included. Evaluation of current commercial actions is very good, particularly now that fewer military actions are readily available.

137. Howe, Walter. **Professional Gunsmithing**. Harrisburg, Pa., Stackpole, 1946. 518p. illus. index. $10.00. LC A48-8110. SBN 8117-1375-X.

An explanatory subtitle to this book is: "A Textbook on the Repair and Alteration of Firearms—with Detailed Notes and Suggestions Relative to the Equipment and Operation of a Commercial Gunshop." At one time, the mortality rate of gunshops was second only to that of jewelry stores, largely due to the inability of the operators to apply sound business principles to their financial affairs. Failure was not necessarily related to their competency as gunsmiths. Although Howe's work is nearly 30 years old, the advice is still sound. He explains how to figure rates of charge, compiling all the factors that must be considered, such as utilities, rent, amortization of tools and equipment, time spent with customers, and the living wage that the gunsmith must have to stay in business. He lists a majority of the tools, supplies, and other stock items essential to the trade, discusses public relations and explains what both the customer and the tradesman have a right to expect from one another. In addition to the business end, there is also a wealth of information on "how-to" gunsmithing to boot. Because of the age of this book, much modernizing of data must be done, but basic principles haven't changed.

138. Kennedy, Monty. **The Checkering and Carving of Gunstocks**. 2nd ed. Harrisburg, Pa., Stackpole, 1962. 336p. illus. $10.00. LC 62-6548. ISBN 0-8117-0630-3.

Man has always decorated his belongings to make them more pleasing to the eye, and gunstocks have been prettied up in one way or another since the early days of gunpowder. Elaborate carving, gold and silver inlays, and jewel encrustations have given way to the simpler, but no less beautiful, carving and checkering, which also serve the utilitarian purpose of making a gun easier to grip firmly. Kennedy, a specialist in the arts of checkering and carving, offers a complete course of study, with patterns and all the "how-to" information needed to begin one's own work. Articles, patterns, comments of many other leading stockmakers and decorators, and photographs of some of the finished products should whet the appetites of do-it-yourselfers. First attempts should be on something other than one's best rifle, however, and much experience and practice is required to gain real proficiency.

139. Linden, Alvin. **Restocking a Rifle**. Harrisburg, Pa., Stackpole, 1969. 139p. illus. patterns. $9.95. LC 69-16152. SBN 8117-1430-6. (One-volume edition of *Firearms Design and Assembly*, which originally appeared in three volumes.)

The late Alvin Linden has been acclaimed as one of the greatest stockmakers in America, and rifles with his stocks are among the prized possessions of their owners. Each of the three volumes gathered together here in one binding still retains its original pagination; the collation above is a total of the three. In each volume, Linden leads the reader through all the steps and tools used in fashioning a stock for a particular gun. First is the 1903 Springfield, second is the Winchester Model 70, and last is the 1917 Enfield. If the would-be stockmaker learns on these three guns, or even on just one, he can adapt the requirements for other rifles with very little trouble. Using salty language, Linden expresses himself quite clearly on such matters as blanks (the block of wood from which the stock is made), the type and quality of various woods, semi-inlets, foreend tips, cheek rests, finishes, etc. The line drawings of blanks and tools and the photographs of the old master himself at his workbench help clarify instructions; the patterns included in a pocket at the back of the book assure the beginner an aesthetically pleasing handle for his smokepole.

140. Walker, Ralph T. **Hobby Gunsmithing.** Northfield, Ill., Digest Books, 1972. 320p. illus. $5.95pa. LC 72-86644. ISBN 0-695-80361-1pa.

Hobby gunsmithing is much like home doctoring: there are many things the amateur can do for himself at low cost, and then there are other matters that require the services of a trained gunsmith or doctor. Critical surgery—the rebarreling or rechambering of a high pressure rifle—requires skill and precision, but refinishing, rebluing, restocking, and a myriad other tasks can be done by the amateur craftsman, with excellent results. The author, a trained, experienced gunsmith, explains many of the "mysteries" of gunsmithing in simple, clear, easy-to-follow instructions. Almost anyone with the interest, a few tools, and effort can do a creditable job, perhaps amazing even himself with the high-quality results.

Antique Firearms

141. Akehurst, Richard. **Sporting Guns**. New York, Putnam's, 1968. 120p. illus. bibliog. $5.95. LC 68-12220. ISBN 0-399-10767-3.

Beginning with the sixteenth century, Akehurst develops the history of firearms and their accessories with text and illustrations—many are beautiful full-color plates, others are black and white photographs. There are a number of facsimiles of illustrations from publications of the past. All illustrations are very well done, and they are the most important part of the volume. At a time when both labor and materials were less costly than at the present, many guns were highly decorated with gold and silver inlays and with engraving on both wood and metal; they were then cased in specially made velvet-lined carrying cases compartmented for the gun and for all the tools necessary to load, clean, and repair that particular gun.

142. Bailey, De Witt. **Percussion Guns and Rifles**. Harrisburg, Pa., Stackpole, 1972. 79p. bibliog. $5.95. LC 72-6794. ISBN 0-8117-1242-7.

This is one of a series of illustrated monographs on arms and armor; there are ten additional titles currently available. The present monograph concerns itself with percussion weapons, following flintlocks and preceding the time of fixed, or self-contained, ammunition. The time span of one type of arm is rather vague, in that flintlocks were used long after the beginning of percussion ignition, and percussion, in turn, was used for many years after the advent of fixed ammunition. Percussion ignition took many forms, from pill lock, tube lock, and other ingenious devices, to the copper cap which fitted over a nipple, the form still used by muzzle loading enthusiasts. The Rev. Forsyth, a Scottish minister, is credited with the invention of the first percussion ignition system soon after the beginning of the nineteenth century. Photographs accompany each numbered entry to describe and show examples of the major variations in rifles using percussion ignition. Distinguishing between smooth bores and rifled bores, the book is divided into sections on sporting guns, sporting rifles, target rifles, military muskets, and military rifles. Most of the arms illustrated are of European manufacture because the leading arms makers of the time were European. The American arms industry had not yet grown to a position of international prominence, and did not do so until rather late in the era of percussion weapons.

143. Boothroyd, Geoffrey. **The Handgun**. New York, Crown, 1970. 564p. illus. index. $19.95. LC 70-108067.

A specialist in the field of handguns, Boothroyd has written one of the most complete histories of handguns to date. The history of handguns, from the earliest and crudest forms to the most modern weapons with the cartridgeless, self-propelling projectiles, presents a fascinating parallel to the advance of civilization and the growing technology in all fields of endeavor. The development of handguns was primarily for military and police purposes; adaptation for sporting use was secondary, until handguns became popular for both hunting and target shooting. This volume is copiously illustrated with excellent photographs and clear, precise descriptions of advances in weaponry; also included are patent drawings for some guns to illustrate significant changes. The major inventors and manufacturers in America and Europe are covered thoroughly, with brief mention of the products of Russia and Japan. The index is extensive and well done, as it must be to service a book this size properly.

144. Butler, David F. **United States Firearms: The First Century, 1776-1875**. New York, Winchester, 1971. 249p. illus. index. $15.00. LC 77-146062. ISBN 0-87691-030-4.

Most firearms in the early days of the United States were flintlocks, and there was little difference between military and non-military weapons except in some of the furnishings, such as bayonets. Designs were basically

European, and many parts were imported. After the revolution, however, the American arms industry began to grow rapidly with ingenious and complex designs being tried. Flintlocks gave way to percussion as more reliable, all-weather ignition was demanded. Breech-loading rifles were developed for flintlocks, but breech loaders did not become very common before the advent of fixed ammunition. Sharpe, Spencer, Colt, Winchester, and Remington all began during the first century of independence, along with a host of others. All left their marks, though many fell by the wayside.

145. Chapel, Charles Edward. **The Gun Collector's Handbook of Values.** 10th ed. New York, Coward, McCann & Geoghegan, 1972. 398p. illus. index. $12.50. LC 72-86474. SBN 698-10503-6.

Begun in 1940 (first copyright date) by the late C. E. Chapel, this price guide is now carried on by his wife, Dorothy M. Chapel, to provide information to both buyers and sellers on the current values of certain American antique firearms. Coverage is best for handguns, both military and commercial, from Revolutionary times forward, although some long guns are included. Prices quoted are for "good" and "fine" according to the description standards of the National Rifle Association. Each gun is described thoroughly to provide identification and some are shown in photographs. The user is warned to be careful of replicas and other fakes which are sometimes offered as the original product. Values shown are subject to change since all are based on supply and demand, and the supply of antique models remains static or decreases as some may be destroyed by fire, lost, or otherwise obliterated. There is included a directory of gunmakers of the flintlock era, a list of freaks and oddities, and short sections on British, French, and other foreign arms. The bulk remains, however, American. Of primary interest to active collectors, institutional and private, this volume might also be of use to individuals seeking to identify family heirlooms.

146. Dunlap, Jack. **American, British, and Continental Pepperbox Firearms**. 2nd ed. Palo Alto, Calif., Pacific Books, 1967. 278p. illus. index. $15.00. LC 64-24121. ISBN 0-87015-158-4.

As a collector and trader for many years, Dunlap specializes in collecting the pepperbox arms he has written about, and he used photographs from his own collection to illustrate this second edition. Ancestors of the modern revolver, pepperboxes had multiple barrels to provide a sequence of shots instead of multiple chambers and a single barrel as do the revolvers we know best. Some pepperboxes were flintlock handguns, some were breech-loading with fixed ammunition, some were shoulder weapons, but most were percussion handguns. There was also a wide variety of mechanisms to accomplish the rotation of the barrels, some were turned by hand, and others did not turn at all. In most examples, the guns were made to fire one shot at a time, but a few touched off all barrels at once to pepper the target literally. The latter type, obviously, set a high value not on accuracy but rather on firepower. Pepperboxes were made and used quite widely, but most casual collectors today know little about them.

147. Glendenning, Ian. **British Pistols and Guns, 1640-1840**. New York, Arco, 1967. 194p. illus. $7.50. LC 67-18416. ISBN 0-668-01646-9. Reprint.

The author describes representative pieces in careful detail to show the development in arms making during the period of 1640 to 1840, the era from which he has chosen to collect. Preceding the main body of the book, he gives a brief history of firearms and the many changes and inventions which affected their manufacture in his chosen time span. He also furnishes an extensive list of names that appear on weapons, with locations and dates of the makers, which will be useful to those who want to identify guns of unknown or questioned origin. In addition to illustrations, each gun is identified by its markings, details of construction, and decoration. A glossary of terms is quite useful, especially for words no longer commonly used with modern arms.

148. Greener, William W. **The Gun and Its Development**. 9th ed. New York, Bonanza, 1967. (Reprint of 1910 ed.) 804p. illus. index. LC 67-27420.

First written in 1881, this is a reprint of the ninth edition, published in 1910. Greener was a famous gunmaker and developer of arms in England, son of William Greener, a gunsmith who had worked for Joe Manton, another great in firearms history. The present work, a massive thing with over 800 pages of smaller-than-average print, discusses the history, development, and uses of arms throughout the world, although English use is the focal point. In working through this tome, it seems that there is not anything that has not been examined in detail that anyone could wish to know about firearms up to the time of the printing. There are many finely detailed drawings, charts, tables of ballistics and other data. Comparisons are made between one manufacturer's product and that of another gunmaker in the same line. Following the index are reproductions of the advertising from the original ninth edition, all ads being for Greener guns or suppliers of powder, ammunition, clothing, etc. There are no ads for guns made by competitors.

149. Lenk, Torsten. **The Flintlock: Its Origin and Development**. Trans. by G. A. Urquhart, ed. by John F. Hayward. New York, Bramhall House, 1965. 188p. illus. bibliog. index. $25.00.

The 15 years of research that went into this study resulted in a doctoral dissertation for Lenk. Acknowledged by many to be the most nearly definitive of all works on flintlocks, it begins with flintlock origins in France in 1610 and carries through to the end of the era, when percussion locks replaced the flint and steel ignition. In addition to the detailed history of the lock and the arm in general, there is also much information on decoration of the weapons—engraving, inlays, and relief carving. Furnishings changed in style with time and with altered needs and purposes. The 134 plates illustrating styles of manufacture and finish are excellent for identification purposes.

150. Lindsay, Merrill. **One Hundred Great Guns: An Illustrated History of Firearms**. New York, Walker, 1967. 379p. illus. bibliog. index. $25.00. LC 67-23653. ISBN 0-8027-0205-8.

A large book heavily illustrated with full-color photographs, this is one of the best in the history of firearms. No exact count was made, but one assumes from the title that there are just one hundred guns discussed and illustrated. Although there are a great many more of some importance in the history of firearms, the author feels that those shown are the most significant as types without getting into the fuzzy area of minor variations. Histories are mostly concerned with developmental stages, but the guns illustrated here could also be very useful to artists and engravers as examples of their arts of the past. The invention of gunpowder came first (and there are several theories as to its origin, none of which will ever be proven definitely); the use of powder in crude weapons followed. Shooters used projectiles such as slugs, shot, even rocks and bits of scrap iron in attempts to improve reliability of the whole combination. A list of "Proof and Control Marks," a list of gunmakers, and a bibliography round out the work.

151. Moore, Warren. **Weapons of the American Revolution . . . and Accoutrements**. New York, Funk & Wagnalls, 1968. 225p. illus. bibliog. $10.00. LC 67-28994.

Plans are underway nationwide to celebrate the two-hundredth anniversary of the American Revolution and the beginning of the new nation. Moore's work should fit in well for planned costumed pageants and parades. Too often books about American history look at only the American side, but Moore covers the small arms used by all participants–American, British, French, and Hessian. The late eighteenth century was a period of change and, although firearms were well established, swords, pikes, sabers, and halberds were still used by some, and metal hat bands to protect against sword slashes were worn by a few as the last vestiges of the armor of an earlier period. Flintlocks were the type of arms used most commonly, and from the American view, most were nonmilitary until the war was well under way, since the colonials had no arms industry to produce in large quantity for a standing army. Rather, each man furnished his hunting-target-home-defense weapon. Military arms were purchased in Europe as soon as possible by the Revolutionary government. Accoutrements include powder horns or flasks, shot pouches, patch cutters and lubricators, ramrods, bayonets, and many other items.

152. Neumann, George C. **The History of Weapons of the American Revolution**. New York, Harper & Row, 1967. 373p. illus. bibliog. index. $15.00. LC 67-20829. ISBN 0-06-071296-1.

Neumann describes the development and changes of small arms prior to and during the American Revolution. The book, designed for reference use, is concise, brief, and to the point. The illustrations by George C. Woodbridge are neither large nor in color but are clear, well captioned, and well organized. The photographs of the arms show the changes, and these illustrations make up the major part of the book. A valuable section in the book is the glossary of terms, which will be useful to the novice because terminology changes with time and with each type of weapon. The book will be most helpful in identifying and classifying weapons during this period in American history; it will be useful not only to the private collector but to museums as well.

153. Russell, Carl P. **Guns on the Early Frontiers: A History of Firearms from Colonial Times through the Years of the Western Fur Trade**. Berkeley, University of California Press, 1962. 395p. illus. bibliog. glossary. index. $2.45pa. LC 57-6042. ISBN 0-520-01105-8pa.

Russell writes from the viewpoint of an historian, which he is, but this work contains much of interest to the gun enthusiast and collector even though his concern with the historical context of the arms may be slight. The subtitle indicates that the book encompasses well over 200 years and a wide range of weapons. The French, Dutch, Spanish, and English all traded in guns, supplying Indians and settlers alike. As the new nation developed and westward expansion began, American gunsmiths made weapons for trade, first using parts imported from Europe, then using parts of wholly American manufacture. The historical impact of varying firepower greatly affected settlement and westward movement.

154. Serven, James E., ed. **The Collecting of Guns**. Harrisburg, Pa., Stackpole, 1964. 272p. illus. bibliog. $24.95 deluxe ed. LC 64-14890. ISBN 0-8117-0381-9.

Thirty-three chapters, written by many different contributors, discuss the very wide field of gun collecting. Very few people realize the vast number of arms makers that have worked in America, or the even more tremendous quantity of models, calibers, styles, and special variations that can attract the attention of a collector of firearms. Serven and the others attempt to explain the why's of guncollecting, which range from a love of history to an interest in mechanics, or possibly just a pecuniary interest. They also discuss many points to be considered other than make or model, such as condition, variations by manufacturers for custom orders, values for special purposes, care and repair of old guns, and how to best preserve and display collections. For either the beginner or the old hand, this volume is invaluable. The photographs, done in sepia tone, are excellent.

155. Taylerson, A. W. F. **The Revolver, 1818-1865**. New York, Crown, 1968. 360p. illus. index. $7.50. LC 68-29115.

Taylerson, A. W. F. **The Revolver, 1865-1888**. New York, Crown, 1966. 202p. illus. index. $7.50. LC 66-18455.

Taylerson, A. W. F. **The Revolver, 1889-1914**. New York, Crown, 1971. 324p. illus. index. $7.50. LC 68-58287.

These three volumes appeared separately, but together they make up a set on the history of the revolver that covers a period of almost 100 years. Perhaps a fourth will be forthcoming to finish up? Arms studied and illustrated are nearly all British or made under British patents, including those of Colt, which were produced in England for a time. Explanations and details are finely drawn; illustrations are photographs. Although constant referral from text to photographs in the appendix makes use somewhat difficult, the reference value to collectors and museums is indispensable. Patent listings, serial number listing for some makers, and much other basic data are given.

156. Trefethen, James B., comp. **Americans and Their Guns**. Ed. by James E. Serven. Harrisburg, Pa., Stackpole, 1967. 320p. illus. index. $9.95. LC 67-12925. ISBN 0-8117-0118-2.

Altogether too many histories, whether of organizations, nations, or even of the world, are dull reading, but Trefethen, of the Wild Life Management Institute, has made this one interesting. The National Rifle Association of America is one of the oldest and certainly the largest of the national organizations concerned with promoting the safe and proper use of firearms. Membership at the present time is in seven figures and is growing rapidly. Past and present membership has included presidents, internationally known military leaders, and many outstanding political and business men. NRA promotes marksmanship among civilians to help prepare men better for military necessities, sponsors police training sessions, international shooting matches, and shooting clubs nationwide. Everyone concerned with shooting and the rights of gun owners should read this book, even though they may oppose the tenets of the NRA.

157. Wilkinson, Frederick. **Antique Firearms**. New York, Doubleday, 1969. 256p. illus. bibliog. index. $10.95. LC 71-93202. ISBN 0-385-05754-7.

This is actually a series of 16 monographs on the history and development of firearms bound into one volume. The author discusses in great detail the history of firearms from the hand cannon down through the development of the percussion lock gun, including Asian, American, and continental guns; flasks and accessories; and manufacturers. Wilkinson treats thoroughly each major stage in their evolution. The facts concerning the earliest history of gunpowder, of course, are still being debated and may never be known precisely. The appeal of the book is enhanced by the excellent quality of photographs, some in color. The indexing is very well done, which makes this volume a useful reference tool.

158. Winant, Lewis. **Early Percussion Firearms: A History of Early Percussion Firearms Ignition–from Forsyth to Winchester .44/40**. New York, Morrow, 1959. 292p. illus. index. $7.50. LC 59-11701.

Percussion ignition, to be technically correct, is the form of ignition used in modern, self-contained ammunition, but general usage speaks of percussion as the follower of flintlock and the precursor of fixed ammunition. Those forms usually included under the percussion heading are the pill lock, caps (hat- or cup-shaped metal containers for fulminate that rested on a nipple), tape, and disk primers. Beginning with the Rev. Alexander Forsyth, first recognized developer of the fulminate primer, Winant leads the reader through the various inventions and attempts to make a reliable ignition system for all kinds of guns. The cap won out as the most practical of the systems, and caps can still be bought today by those who enjoy shooting the old muzzle loaders. Photographs illustrating guns using the several systems are clear and well done.

Single Makers

WINCHESTER

159. Butler, David F. **Winchester '73 & '76: The First Repeating Centerfire Rifles**. New York, Winchester, 1970. 95p. illus. $7.95. LC 71-99754. SBN 87691-015-0.

Following Parsons' *The First Winchester* (next entry), Butler considers the models of 1873 and 1876, both in historical perspective and as arms for the collector. The 1873 was, and probably still is, the best known of all the early rifles of the American frontier; many are still in use in some of the western states. The '76 was the big brother of the '73—essentially the same in appearance and mechanism, but larger and using more powerful ammunition. The '73 was manufactured for a total of 51 or 52 years, while the '76 was discontinued after about 20 years of production.

160. Parsons, John E. **The First Winchester: The Story of the 1866 Repeating Rifle**. Rev. ed. New York, Winchester, 1969. 207p. illus. index. $8.95. LC 60-12290.

Williamson's *Winchester, the Gun that Won the West* (entry 162) related the business and economic history of the Winchester Company, but provided relatively little information about the arms themselves for the benefit of the collector. This lack was the basis of Parsons' work, whose aim is to present the first Winchester and its forerunners to collectors and historians. The 1866 Winchester, which followed the Henry rifle, used the same cartridge, the .44 Henry Flat, a rimfire cartridge. With the exception of .22 calibers, all other Winchesters since the 1866 have fired center fire ammunition. This volume is a "must" for all Winchester aficionados; it is followed, chronologically, by Butler's work (entry 159).

161. Watrous, George R. **The History of Winchester Firearms, 1866-1966.** 3rd ed. Ed. by Thomas E. Hall and Pete Kuhlhoff. New York, Winchester, 1966. 159p. illus. $10.00. LC 66-25540.

Originally compiled by Watrous, a Winchester employee, for in-house use, this is a record of all Winchester arms and their forerunners with which Oliver Winchester was associated. Arranged in chronological sequence, each gun is described with general specifications and placed in historical perspective. Manufacturing history, total numbers produced, and the calibers chambered in each model make this compilation very important to collectors and museums. Although some variations in each model may be noted, customized special orders were much more common years ago than today, therefore not *all* special variations are listed.

162. Williamson, Harold F. **Winchester, the Gun that Won the West.** Washington, Combat Forces Press, 1952. 494p. illus. index. $10.00. LC 52-11409. Encore Reprint, Barnes, $5.98. ISBN 0-498-08315-2.

The title of this work is, or could be, somewhat misleading in that it is the economic history, or business history of the Winchester Company rather than a history of the arms themselves, which are considered only incidentally. Williamson was a professor of economic history at Northwestern University at the time of writing. Winchester Repeating Arms Co. and/or its predecessors that evolved into WRA has gone through seven or eight wars and several depressions; it is still a lively, viable company, although now a part of Olin Corporation. A company history is much more than a series of balance sheets; it involves the lives and personalities of people both within and without the company. It also involves competitors, the U.S. government, and international affairs.

COLT

163. Parsons, John E. **The Peacemaker and Its Rivals: An Account of the Single Action Colt**. New York, Morrow, 1950. 184p. illus. index. $7.50. LC 50-9423.

Beginning with the revolvers that preceded the single action Colt, Parsons describes the evolution of the pistol that has retained its popularity for 100 years and has been copied by other manufacturers. Known also as a "Thumbbuster" because some shooters held the trigger back and worked the action by repeatedly thumbing the hammer, the Peacemaker came out in 1873. It was made continuously until about the beginning of World War II, when it was discontinued, but popular demand revived it and it can now be purchased in essentially its original form. Chambered at various times for the .32-20, .38-40, .44-40, and .45 calibers, it was a favorite of men who carried rifles chambered for the first three cartridges. One belt of ammunition could be used in either weapon. The U.S. Army adopted the Peacemaker and received shipments each year from 1874 through 1893, when it was replaced in the official list. An extremely useful list on pages 86 and 87 gives the serial number range and annual production for each year from 1873 through 1940. Collectors and museums can tell the date of manufacture of their weapons if the number is below 357,859.

SMITH & WESSON

164. Neal, Robert J., and Roy G. Jinks. **Smith and Wesson, 1857-1945**. New York, Barnes, 1966. 360p. illus. bibliog. index. $25.00. LC 66-12902. ISBN 0-498-06377-1.

Smith & Wesson is an old company which in many ways has grown up with the nation. The authors list the arms produced since the inception of the firm, describe and illustrate them up to the end of World War II. Organization is by caliber, then by the chronology of manufacture. Many gun makers provided custom service for buyers, installing special grips and stocks, special engraving, non-standard sighting equipment and other features for which the customers were willing to pay. These variations make it difficult for a researcher to identify positively every item produced, and Neal and Jinks are aware that many may have been missed. The lack of accurate records makes it difficult for dealers and collectors to be certain that non-standard guns are factory produced and not customized at some later date, a factor that may affect pricing, especially for antiques. Identification aids, drawings from patent applications, and X-ray photos are in an appendix.

Chapter 6

ARCHERY

165. Gillelan, G. Howard. **Complete Book of the Bow and Arrow.** Harrisburg, Pa., Stackpole, 1971. 320p. illus. index. $9.95. LC 72-140739. SBN 8117-0420-3.

By the editor of the archery column of *Outdoor Life* magazine, this is archery as it is today, with excerpts from the rules of the National Archery Association, Fédération Internationale de Tir à l'Arc (International Archery Federation), and the National Field Archery Association. Beginning with a history of archery, major developments in equipment are discussed, and many of the new ideas really are not so new after all. The laminated, recurved bow of current popularity was used by Turks, Persians, and some American Indians centuries ago, although their materials were inferior to modern laminates. While arrow shafts of wood are still used extensively, shafts of aluminum and fiberglass are superior in many respects. According to the author, the modern bow is more closely related to those of the Persians than to the famous English longbows of Robin Hood fame. All gear is mentioned–quivers, arm guards, sights, stabilizers, etc.–and their values are compared when used in various conditions such as hunting versus field archery versus target (range) archery. Brand names and products are not rated. Bowhunting and bowfishing, as growing sports, receive their fair amount of attention, as do the archery associations that seek to promote the sport in both hunting and competition. A glossary of terms, a complete table of contents, and a good index make this an excellent reference volume.

166. Heath, E. G. **The Grey Goose Wing.** New York, New York Graphic Society, 1972. 352p. illus. bibliog. index. $24.95. LC 75-183970. ISBN 0-8212-0449-1.

The title, which refers to the grey goose wing-feathers that arrow-makers used for fletchings, is quite appropriate for a history of archery. There are many narratives of people and of battles in which the long bow was the primary weapon. Bows and arrows have been in use for centuries, being referred to in the Bible, and are still in use as weapons by some primitive cultures and as sporting arms by hunters and target shooters throughout the world. Terminology is explained as needed in the text, but a separate glossary would probably have been a worthwhile addition. Bibliographies follow each chapter. The 350 illustrations, part in color, are well done. An excellent reference work.

167. Schuyler, Keith C. **Archery: From Golds to Big Game**. New York, Barnes, 1970. 569p. photos. index. $12.00. LC 70-88292. ISBN 0-498-06961-3.

Schuyler gives a brief but thorough history of archery and contrasts the past with the present to emphasize the technological progress in equipment. He provides excellent coverage of national and international organizations, their rules, their tournaments, and the prizes offered. In the hunting aspect, archers seek fish, birds, snakes, and all types of large and small game. Illustrations are photographs made by the author. The growing sport of archery is attracting more and more participants each year as many feel that the bow more nearly puts the hunter on even terms with his game. The archer certainly needs more skill in stalking game than does the rifleman because of the difference in ranges from which killing shots may be made. Target practice with the bow can also be carried on in densely populated areas where the use of a rifle would be unsafe.

168. Wambold, Homer R. **Bowhunting for Deer**. Harrisburg, Pa., Stackpole, 1964. 160p. illus. $5.95. LC 64-21466. ISBN 0-8117-0293-6.

Hunters who choose a bow as their weapon over a rifle are growing in numbers, but literature for the bowhunter is still in relatively short supply. Wambold is a Pennsylvania whitetail hunter with sound instruction and advice for archers after deer. Those who go after mule deer in the open country of the West may have a lot of adapting to do, but the equipment recommendations will still be valuable. The beginning archer is advised on bow selection, arrow matching, quivers, and other accessories.

Tips are given with no axe to grind, whereas the salesman of sporting goods may be overly enthusiastic about his products but have little practical knowledge of the sport. After selection is made and proficiency is gained through much practice, a study of the game is in order. The author discusses whitetail and their habits and anatomy to instruct in hunting procedures, target areas, the unorthodox positions for shooting that invariably arise, and the care of game after the kill, including recipes for preparation of the meat. Organizations for the bow hunter are growing across the country, so the Pope and Young Club is now maintaining records similar to the Boone and Crockett Club records for rifle hunters.

Chapter 7

PERIODICALS

The following is a selected list of periodicals with wide circulation. Many others of regional or local interest have not been included. The game and fish departments or conservation departments of most states publish regular periodicals on hunting, fishing, wildlife, boating, camping, or conservation that is of most interest to the residents of the state. These are usually available for a nominal fee and should be searched out and supported by sportsmen.

169. **American Cooner**. George O. Slankard, ed. and pub., 114-120 Franklin Avenue, Sesser, Ill. 62884. Monthly. $4.00 per year.

Devoted to coon hounds and coon hunting. Information on breeding, selection, training, and running of hounds.

170. **American Rifleman**. National Rifle Association of America, 1600 Rhode Island Avenue, N.W., Washington, D.C. 20036. Monthly. Membership and journal $7.50 per year.

Official publication of the NRA, carrying articles on firearms, legislation, gunsmithing, and hunting. Special sections on new products and test results, shooting data, tournament events, life memberships, and necrology. Extensive classified ad section. Advertisers are monitored to assure reliability.

171. **Archery World**. H. Lee Schwanz, pub., 534 North Broadway, Milwaukee, Wis. 53202. Bimonthly. $3.00 per year.

Wide coverage of articles and news of interest to archers, both hunting and target enthusiasts.

172. **Bow and Arrow**. Gallant Publishing Company, 116 E. Badillo Street, Covina, Calif. 91722. Bimonthly. $3.00 per year.

Popular publication on archery, hunting and fishing with bow and arrow, and articles and news on new equipment. Published by the same firm that puts out *Gun World*.

173. **The Chase**. Chase Publishing Company, Inc., 1140 Industry Road, Lexington, Ky. 40505. Monthly. $3.50 per year.

Official publication of the National Fox Hunting Association. Articles on fox hunting and on the breeding, care, selection, and training of fox hounds.

174. **Field & Stream**. Holt, Rinehart & Winston, Inc., 383 Madison Avenue, New York, N.Y. 10017. Monthly. $5.00 per year.

Articles and columns on hunting, fishing, boating, dogs, firearms, archery, camping. Regular features on most of these in addition to the stories of personal experiences of various writers. Advertising. One of the leading popular outdoor magazines.

175. **Fishing & Hunting News**. P.O. Box 3504, Terminal Annex, Seattle, Wash. 98124. Weekly. $5.00 per year.

Largely restricted to hunting and fishing in the western United States. Articles, news items, stories.

176. **Full Cry**. Walker Publishing Company, Box 190, Sedalia, Mo. 65301. Monthly. $4.00 per year.

As the title would indicate, the interest is in free hounds, coon hounds, and hunting with hounds.

177. **Fur-Fish-Game**. A. R. Harding Publishing Company, 2878 E. Main Street, Columbus, Ohio 43209. Monthly. $4.00 per year.

Contains articles on hunting, fishing, trapping, camping, boating. There are regular columns on travel, conservation, fishing and tackle, and hunting. There is also a question and answer column and a classified ad section.

178. **Gun Sport & Gun Collector**. Leisure Publishing, Inc., The Clark Bldg., Pittsburgh, Pa. 15222. Monthly. $7.50 per year.

Although articles are scattered throughout the magazine, the index classifies them under the headings of handguns, rifles, shotguns, hunting, handloading, black powder, knives, and collecting. There is a section on new products, and a classified ad section.

179. **Gun Week**. 119 East Court Street, Sidney, Ohio 45365. Weekly. $5.00 per year.

Of interest both to shooters and to collectors. Carries articles on shooting, on antique guns and collecting of guns, and on legislation that affects gun owners.

180. **Gun World**. Gallant Publishing Company, Inc., 116 E. Badillo Street, Covina, Calif. 91722. Monthly. $6.00 per year.

Publishes features and columns on almost every facet of guns and the shooting sports, including items of interest to collectors and hunters.

181. **Guns & Ammo**. Petersen Publishing Company, 8490 Sunset Blvd., Los Angeles, Calif. 90069. Monthly. $7.50 per year.

Articles on hunting, shooting, collecting, and general information of value to the gun owner and shooter. Regular departments on legislation, correspondence, gunsmithing, new products and tests.

182. **Guns and Game**. Stanley Publications, Inc., 261 Fifth Avenue, New York, N.Y. 10016. Bimonthly. $4.50 per year.

Publishes articles and stories on hunting with firearms. Presents technical data on guns, cartridges, loading of ammunition, barrels, actions, accessories, etc. Regular departments are on gunsmithing, ballistics, and reloading.

183. **Guns Magazine**. Publishers' Development Corp., 8150 N. Central Park Avenue, Skokie, Ill. 60076. Monthly. $7.50 per year.

Demonstrates a wide range of interest in the firearms and shooting field, with articles on collecting, hunting, target shooting, and studies of individual weapons. Regular columns on handgunning, muzzle-loading weapons and shooting, trap and skeet, and legislation.

184. **Hunter's Horn**. Hunter's Horn, Inc., 8200 Charles Pages Blvd., Sand Springs, Okla. 74063. Monthly. $4.00 per year.

Designed for the use of foxhound owners who hunt fox, wolf, coyote, and the cats–bob cats, lynx, and mountain lion. Articles on foxhound breeding, training, care, and hunting. Also information on field trials and shows.

185. **Muzzle Blasts**. National Muzzle Loading Rifle Association, Box 67, Friendship, Ind. 47021. Monthly. $6.00 per year with membership.

Official organ of the NMLRA, articles are of interest to those enthusiasts who own and shoot the old muzzle loaders or the new replicas. Loading information, hunting news, legislation, accessories used by muzzle loaders, and target match news are all carried.

186. **Outdoor Life**. Popular Science Publishing Company, Inc., 355 Lexington Avenue, New York, N.Y. 10017. Monthly. $5.00 per year.

Another of the leading outdoor magazines, this one carries articles on hunting, fishing, camping, travel, boating. Regular departments on each in addition to the stories involving the above activities. Sponsors the Outdoor Life Book Club to publish books, mostly on hunting, fishing, and firearms.

187. **Rod & Gun in Canada**. Rod & Gun Publishing Corp., 1219 Hotel de Ville, Montreal, Quebec, Canada. Monthly. Canadian $3.00, U.S. $4.00 per year.

Illustrated stories on Canadian wildlife, hunting, fishing, camping, travel, conservation, and boating.

188. **Salt-Water Sportsman**. Salt Water Sportsman, Inc., 10 High Street, Boston, Mass. 02110. Monthly. $5.00 per year.

Published for the benefit of salt-water fishermen with the greatest appeal in the coastal areas. Articles on fishing the salt-water areas of close-by neighboring countries such as Canada, the Bahamas, and coastal areas of Mexico.

189. **Shooting Times**. Peoria Journal Star, Inc., News Plaza, Peoria, Ill. 61601. Monthly. $5.85 per year.

Shooting Times contains articles on every form of shooting, plus data on tests made on new guns and accessories, legislative reports, and regular columns on loading, conservation, gunsmithing, and shoppers information.

190. **The Shotgun News.** Box 1147, Hastings, Neb. 68901. Semi-monthly. $5.00 per year.

Classified advertising newspaper, tabloid size. Lists thousands of ads each issue from individuals and firms who are buyers, traders, or sellers. Regular study of the ads will give a good idea of current market prices for most items.

191. **Skeet Shooting Review.** National Skeet Shooting Association, 2608 Inwood Road, Dallas, Tex. 75235. Monthly. $5.00 per year.

Articles on skeet shooting with competition records and data, tournament events, and Association activities.

192. **Sports Afield.** Hearst Magazines, 250 West 55th Street, New York, N.Y. 10022. Monthly. $5.00 per year.

One of the top three in general outdoor sports magazines, *Sports Afield* contains articles and regular columns on hunting, fishing, boating, camping, firearms, and conservation.

193. **Trap & Field.** Review Publishing Company, Inc., 1100 Waterway Blvd., Indianapolis, Ind. 46202. Monthly, except semi-monthly in March. $7.00 per year.

Official publication of the Amateur Trapshooting Association. Publishes articles and instruction on trapshooting, reports on competitive matches and scores, publicizes matches.

194. **Western Fish & Game.** Western Fish & Game Magazine Ltd., 1020 Hornby Street, Vancouver, British Columbia, Canada. Bimonthly. Canadian $3.50, U.S. $5.00 per year.

Articles and news of fishing and hunting in western Canada.

Chapter 8

NATIONAL ORGANIZATIONS

Most national organizations have local chapters wherever there are enough individuals to organize and support the national's goals. Joining, or even organizing, a local chapter is an excellent way to meet others with like interests. For a newcomer to a community or for a beginner in a sport, it is perhaps the best way to make friends, gain congenial companions, and to learn about the sporting opportunities available in the area. Supporting local and national organizations helps promote the activities and ideals of the individual.

ARCHERY

American Archery Council, R.D. 1, Box 119, Bechtelsville, Pa. 19505.

For persons interested in the sport of archery, and for dealers and suppliers of archery equipment. Tries to promote archery and widen its appeal. Holds an annual meeting and tournament.

American Indoor Archery Association, Box 174, Grayling, Mich. 49738.

Established to develop rules for indoor shooting. Commercial lanes, similar to bowling lanes, are in operation in some areas and competitive leagues are being formed. This organization promotes practice throughout the year, especially when weather prevents outdoor activity.

National Archery Association of the United States, 2833 Lincoln Hwy., E., Ronks, Pa. 17572.

Organization of individuals and affiliated clubs interested primarily in target archery. Standardizes rules and regulations, maintains official records. Sponsors annual national championship tournament, other tournaments, and awards medals. Publishes *TAM/Archery World* monthly.

National Field Archery Association, Route 2, Box 514, Redlands, Calif. 92373.

This is the largest of the various archery associations and is a federation of state and local clubs. For field archers and bowhunters, the local clubs sponsor archery schools and regional and national tournaments, and compile reports on hunting. The Association works for conservation. Publishes *Archery* monthly.

Professional Archers Association, 1500 N. Chatsworth Street, St. Paul, Minn. 55117.

An organization of competitive archers and instructors of archery. Sponsors professional tournaments and holds an annual convention.

HUNTING AND SHOOTING

Amateur Trapshooting Association, P.O. Box 246, West National Road, Vandalia, Ohio 45377.

Promotes the sport of trapshooting, publishes rules and regulations for shoots, maintains records for each shooter, and sponsors the Grand American Trapshooting Tournament annually in Vandalia. Maintains an historical exhibit and a Hall of Fame. Publishes *Trap and Field* magazine monthly.

American Coon Hunters Association, c/o Mr. Raymond McClure, West Point, Miss. 39773.

For those interested in coon dogs and coon hunting. An annual field championship competition for coon dogs is held.

American Single Shot Rifle Association, 13 East Prospect Avenue, Mount Prospect, Ill. 60056.

This is a small group interested in the use and study of single shot rifles produced between the end of the Civil War and the beginning of World War I. It sponsors shooting competitions and publishes *American Single Shot Rifle News* bimonthly.

Association of American Rod and Gun Clubs in Europe, OCPA, Headquarters USAREUR/7A, APO New York, N.Y. 09403.

An affiliation of rod and gun clubs connected with military organizations in Europe, North Africa, and the Near East with the purpose of promoting all the field sports—hunting, fishing, archery, trap, skeet, etc. Publishes *Rod and Gun* monthly.

National Bench Rest Shooters Association, 607 West Line Street, Minerva, Ohio 44657.

Precision target shooters will be interested in this group of like-minded gunners. They hold meets and competitions, and maintain records. Publishes *Precision Shooting* monthly.

National Board for the Promotion of Rifle Practice, Forrestal Bldg. (West), Room 1J057, Washington, D.C. 20310.

An organization of the U.S. Army set up to promote rifle practice and marksmanship among civilians. The board provides arms and ammunition to member clubs, maintains records, provides awards for competitions.

National Fox Hunters Association, P.O. Box 1806, Jackson, Tenn. 38301.

The NFHA has individual members as well as affiliated local and state clubs. It sponsors field trials for fox hounds, regular shows, and horse shows, since horses are used extensively in fox hunting. Publishes *The Chase* monthly.

National Muzzle Loading Rifle Association, Friendship, Ind. 47021.

As the title indicates, the interest of this group is in the muzzle-loading weapons of the past and, presumably, of the present in the form of newly manufactured replicas. Maintains a range in Friendship and sponsors three competitive shoots each year. Publishes *Muzzle Blasts* monthly.

National Rifle Association of America, 1600 Rhode Island Avenue, N.W., Washington, D.C. 20036.

Largest of the shooting organizations, the NRA has well over one million members. Promotes safety, marksmanship, conservation. Maintains extensive records on shooting matches, laws, affiliated clubs. Sponsors matches, both local and national. Publishes *The American Rifleman* monthly as its official journal and *Tournament News* monthly for match dates and records.

National Shooting Sports Foundation, 1075 Post Road, Riverside, Conn. 06878.

Although this organization is not open to the individual shooter, he should be aware of its existence and activities. It is composed of manufacturers of guns, ammunition, components, accessories, etc., and publishers of hunting and shooting oriented periodicals. The Foundation seeks to promote the shooting sports, safety, and sensible legislation, and it publishes pamphlets and reports concerning its interests. Its activities are important to all sportsmen.

National Skeet Shooting Association, 3409 Oak Lawn Avenue, Dallas, Tex. 75219.

This organization for amateur shooters of skeet sponsors competitive shoots, makes and publishes rules, maintains records. Monthly publication is *Skeet Shooting Review*.

North-South Skirmish Association, 5279 Case Avenue, Lundhurst, Ohio 44124.

Organized to perpetuate the memory of the soldiers in the Civil War on both sides. Holds matches with participants dressed in the uniforms of the Civil War and using Civil War weapons. Publishes *Skirmish Line* magazine bimonthly. A national organization, but the major appeal is regional, east of the Mississippi.

Pacific International Trapshooting Association, 7480 Aumsville Hwy., S.E., Salem, Ore. 97301.

Promotes trapshooting and sponsors shoots. Maintains records, but has no regular publication.

Shooters Club of America, 8150 North Central Park Avenue, Skokie, Ill. 60076.

A relatively young organization, it is open to everyone interested in maintaining the right of Americans to keep and bear arms for legitimate purposes. Carries on educational programs to help combat restrictive anti-gun legislation at all levels of government. Publishes the *Shooters Club Newsletter* quarterly.

United States Revolver Association, 59 Alvin Street, Springfield, Mass. 01104.

Promotes revolver and pistol shooting and marksmanship by encouraging competitive matches and maintaining records. Publishes *U.S. Handgunner* monthly.

FISHING

American Casting Association, P.O. Box 51, Nashville, Tenn. 37202.

A federation of organizations of fly and bait casters, the Association sponsors competitive matches, maintains records, publishes rules, and works to promote casting as a recreational sport. Publishes *Creel* bimonthly.

Association of Surf Angling Clubs, 1301 Wyngate Road, Wynnewood, Pa. 19096.

These federated surf-fishing clubs work for better laws to reduce or prohibit pollution of coastal waters, and for conservation of ocean fish and game. They promote tournaments, compile rules, make awards, and maintain records.

Caribbean Gamefishing Association, P.O. Box 366, Coral Gables, Fla. 33134.

Limiting its interest to the Caribbean, it provides its members with information on that area, maintains records, cooperates in scientific research endeavors, and publishes *CGA News* monthly.

International Women's Fishing Association, P.O. Box 2025, Palm Beach, Fla. 33480.

Although this is a small organization, it is unique in that it is for women only. It promotes sportsmanship among women, gives awards for fishing accomplishments, and encourages conservation. Publishes *Hooks and Lines* monthly.

Chapter 9

PUBLISHERS

The publishers of the books included in this volume are to be commended for consistently high quality in typography, photographic reproduction, and binding. Most of the presses represented are old, experienced firms, but others are young and working hard to establish themselves and their reputations. Many of the outdoors books cost more to produce than novels because of the amount of illustrative material they include, which is expensive to reproduce, especially when it is in full color. The ultimate cost to the buyer is thus sometimes rather high, but Americans have always been willing to pay a fair price for top quality merchandise, whether it be clothing, food, or books. Books are still a good buy and a good investment.

Arco Publishing Co., Inc.
219 Park Avenue South
New York, New York 10003

A. S. Barnes & Co.
Forsgate Drive
Cranbury, New Jersey 08512

Barre Publishers
South Street
Barre, Massachusetts 01005

Bonanza Press
Box 2037
Santa Cruz, California 95060

Century House, Inc.
Watkins Glen,
New York 14891

Combat Forces Press
See A. S. Barnes & Co.

Cord Communications
Simon and Schuster, Inc.
630 Fifth Avenue
New York, New York 10020

Coward, McCann & Geohegan, Inc.
200 Madison Avenue
New York, New York 10016

Thomas Y. Crowell Co.
Subsidiary of Dun & Bradstreet, Inc.
666 Fifth Avenue
New York, New York 10019

Crown Publishers, Inc.
419 Park Avenue South
New York, New York 10016

Digest Books, Inc.
540 Frontage Road
Northfield, Illinois 60093

Dillon Press
106 Washington Avenue N.
Minneapolis, Minnesota 55401

Dodd, Mead & Co.
79 Madison Avenue
New York, New York 10016

Doubleday & Co., Inc.
277 Park Avenue
New York, New York 10017

E. P. Dutton & Co., Inc.
201 Park Avenue South
New York, New York 10003

Fireside Books
Div. of Warren H. Green, Inc.
10 South Brentwood Blvd.
St. Louis, Missouri 63105

Follett Publishing Co.
Div. of Follett Corp.
1010 Washington Blvd.
Chicago, Illinois 60607

Funk & Wagnalls Publishing Co.
Subsidiary of Thomas Y. Crowell Co.
666 Fifth Avenue
New York, New York 10019

Golden Press
See Western Publishing Co.

Great Outdoors Publishing Co.
4747 28 Street N
St. Petersburg, Florida 33714

Harper & Row, Publishers
10 East 53 Street
New York, New York 10022

Houghton Mifflin Co.
2 Park Street
Boston, Massachusetts 02107

International Marine Publishing Co.
Subsidiary of Journal Publications, Inc.
21 Elm Street
Camden, Maine 04843

Jenkins Book Publishing Co.
Box 2085
Austin, Texas 78767

Alfred A. Knopf
Subsidiary of Random House, Inc.
201 East 50 Street
New York, New York 10022

Lane Magazine & Book Co.
Menlo Park,
California 94025

Lansdowne Press Pty. Ltd.
380 Bourke Street
Melbourne, Australia
Distributed by: Sportshelf

J. B. Lippincott Co.
East Washington Square
Philadelphia, Pennsylvania 19105

Little, Brown & Co.
34 Beacon Street
Boston, Massachusetts 02106

Livingston Publishing Company
18 Hampstead Circle
Wynnewood, Pennsylvania 19096

The Macmillan Co.
Subsidiary of Crowell Collier & Macmillan, Inc.
866 Third Avenue
New York, New York 10022

Maco Publications
Simon & Schuster, Inc.
630 Fifth Avenue
New York, New York 10020

William Morrow & Co., Inc.
Subsidiary of Scott, Foresman & Co.
105 Madison Avenue
New York, New York 10016

Mountain Press
279-287 West Front Street
Missoula, Montana 59801

Naylor Company
1015 Culebra Avenue
Box 1838
San Antonio, Texas 78201

R. W. Norton Art Gallery
4747 Creswell Avenue
Shreveport, Louisiana 71106

Outdoor Life
Distributed by other presses:
Outdoor Life/Harper,
Outdoor Life/Doubleday,
etc.

Pacific Books, Publishers
Box 558
Palo Alto, California 94302

Penguin Books, Inc.
7110 Ambassador Road
Baltimore, Maryland 21207

Petersen Publishing Company
8490 Sunset Blvd.
Los Angeles, California 90069

Pocket Books, Inc.
Div. of Simon & Schuster, Inc.
630 Fifth Avenue
New York, New York 10020

G. P. Putnam's Sons
200 Madison Avenue
New York, New York 10016

Random House, Inc.
Subsidiary of Radio Corporation of America
201 East 50 Street
New York, New York 10022

Henry Regnery Company
114 W. Illinois Street
Chicago, Illinois 60610

Ridge Press, Inc.
Aff. with Rutledge Books, Inc.
17 East 45 Street
New York, New York 10017

Charles Scribner's Sons
597 Fifth Avenue
New York, New York 10017

Simon & Schuster, Inc.
630 Fifth Avenue
New York, New York 10020

Sportshelf
P.O. Box 634
New Rochelle, New York 10802

Stackpole Company
Cameron and Kelker Streets
Harrisburg, Pennsylvania 17105

Stoeger Arms Corp.
55 Ruta Court
South Hackensack, New Jersey 07606

Charles E. Tuttle Company
28 South Main Street
Rutland, Vermont, 05701

University of California Press
2223 Fulton Street
Berkeley, California 94720

Van Nostrand Reinhold Co.
Div. of Litton Educational Publishing, Inc.
450 West 33 Street
New York, New York 10001

Walker & Company
Div. of Walker Publishing Co., Inc.
720 Fifth Avenue
New York, New York 10019

Western Publishing Co., Inc.
1220 Mound Avenue
Racine, Wisconsin 53404

Winchester Press
Div. of Olin Corporation
460 Park Avenue
New York, New York 10022

Chapter 10

DIRECTORY OF MANUFACTURERS AND SUPPLIERS

When purchasing fishing tackle, hunting equipment, archery supplies, and all the needed accessories, the sportsman's first stop should be at the local sporting goods dealer. By buying locally, the buyer has the opportunity to see and handle the merchandise, to inspect it for quality and suitability. If a warranty is involved and an adjustment must be made, results can be obtained more quickly person-to-person than through correspondence with some far-off supplier. Many of the products manufactured by firms included in the selected list can also be purchased locally. The list is provided as a supplement to the holdings of local dealers and for the benefit of those who may live some distance from a merchant with a good stock.

Hunting and Shooting

AMMUNITION (COMMERCIAL)

Federal Cartridge Company
2700 Foshay Tower
Minneapolis, Minnesota 55402

Omark-CCI, Inc.
Box 856
Lewiston, Idaho 83501

Remington Arms Company
Bridgeport, Connecticut 06602

Smith & Wesson-Fiocchi, Inc.
3640 Seminary Road
Alton, Illinois 62002

Speer-DWM
Box 896
Lewiston, Idaho 83501

Weatherby's
2781 East Firestone Blvd.
South Gate, California 90280

Winchester-Western
East Alton, Illinois 62024

AMMUNITION (CUSTOM)

Ammodyne
Box 1589
Los Angeles, California 90053

Bill Ballard
P.O. Box 656
Billings, Montana 59103

Caldwell's Loading Service
1314 Monroe Drive, N.E.
Atlanta, Georgia 30306

Ellwood Epps
80 King Street
Clinton, Ontario, Canada

Mansfield Gunshop
Box 83
New Boston, New Hampshire 03070

Numrich Arms Corp.
203 Broadway
West Hurley, New York 12491

Wanda Cartridge Company
P.O. Box 45901
Houston, Texas 77045

Whitney Cartridge Company
Box 5872
Pasadena, California 91107

AMMUNITION (FOREIGN)

Abercrombie & Fitch
Madison at 45th Street
New York, New York 10017

Canadian Industries, Ltd.
Box 10
Montreal, Quebec, Canada

Centennial Arms Company
3318 West Devon Avenue
Chicago, Illinois 60645

DWM, Speer Products, Inc.
Box 641
Lewiston, Idaho 83501

Norma-Precision
South Lansing, New York 14882

Stoeger Arms Corp.
55 Ruta Court
South Hackensack, New Jersey
07606

AMMUNITION (LOADING COMPONENTS)

Belding & Mull
107 North Fourth Street
Philipsburg, Pennsylvania 16866

C-H Tool & Die Corp.
Owen, Wisconsin 54460

Du Pont
Explosives Dept.
Wilmington, Delaware 19898

Hercules Powder Company
910 Market Street
Wilmington, Delaware 19899

Herter's Inc.
Waseca, Minnesota 56093

Hornaday Mfg. Company
Box 1848
Grand Island, Nebraska 68801

Lee's Precision Bullets
4474 Yosemite Way
Los Angeles, California 90065

Lyman Gun Sight Products
Middlefield, Connecticut 06455

Mayville Engineering Co., Inc.
Mayville, Wisconsin 53050

Norma-Precision
South Lansing, New York 14482

Nosler Bullets
P.O. Box 688
Beaverton, Oregon 97005

Pacific Tool Company
P.O. Drawer 2048
Ordnance Plant Road
Grand Island, Nebraska 68801

RCBS, Inc.
P.O. Box 1919
Oroville, California 95965

Remington-Peters
Bridgeport, Connecticut
06602

Sierra Bullets, Inc.
421 North Altadena Drive
Pasadena, California 91107

Smith & Wesson-Fiocchi, Inc.
3640 Seminary Road
Alton, Illinois 62002

Speer Products, Inc.
Box 896
Lewiston, Idaho 83501

Winchester-Western
New Haven, Connecticut
06504

ANTIQUE ARMS DEALERS

Robert Abels
157 East 64th Street
New York, New York 10021

Francis Bannerman's Sons, Inc.
Box 126
Blue Point, Long Island,
New York 11715

Ellwood Epps
80 King Street
Clinton, Ontario, Canada

Farris Muzzle Guns
1610 Gallia Street
Portsmouth, Ohio 45662

N. Flayderman & Company
4 Squash Hollow
New Milford, Connecticut 06776

Herb Glass
Bullville, New York 10915

Heritage Firearms Company
27 Danbury Road
Route 7
Wilton, Connecticut 06897

Holbrook Arms Museum
12953 Biscayne Blvd.
North Miami, Florida 33161

Ed Howe
2 Main
Coopers Mills, Maine 04341

Jackson Arms
6209 Hillcrest Avenue
Dallas, Texas 75205

Museum of Historical Arms
1038 Alton Road
Miami Beach, Florida 33139

National Gun Traders, Inc.
Box 776
Miami, Florida 33135

New Orleans Arms Co., Inc.
240 Chartres Street
New Orleans, Louisiana 70130

Martin B. Retting, Inc.
11029 Washington
Culver City, California 90230

Santa Ana Gunroom
1638 East 1st Street
Santa Ana, California 92701

GAME CALLS

Burnham Bros.
Box 100-C
Marble Falls, Texas 78654

Lohman Mfg. Co.
320 East Spring
Neosho, Missouri 64850

Phillip S. Olt Co.
Box 550
Pekin, Illinois 61554

Weems Wild Calls
Box 7261
Fort Worth, Texas 76111

GUN PARTS, U.S. AND FOREIGN

Badger Shooter's Supply
Owen, Wisconsin 54460

Shelley Braverman
Athens, New York 12015

Hunter's Haven
Zero Prince Street
Alexandria, Virginia 22314

Numrich Arms Company
West Hurley, New York 12491

Pacific International Import Co.
2416 16th Street
Sacramento, California 95818

Reed & Company
Shokan, New York 12481

Martin B. Retting, Inc.
11029 Washington
Culver City, California 90230

N. F. Strebe
4926 Marlboro Pike, S.E.
Washington, D.C. 20027

GUNS (AMERICAN MADE)

American Firearms Mfg. Co., Inc.
5732 Kenwick Drive
San Antonio, Texas 78238

Benjamin Air Rifle Company
855 Marion Street
St. Louis, Missouri 63104

Champlin Firearms, Inc.
Box 3191
Enid, Oklahoma 73701

Colt's
150 Huyshope Avenue
Hartford, Connecticut 06102

Firearms Development, Inc.
218 Austin Street
Denton, Texas 76201

Harrington & Richardson
Park Avenue
Worcester, Massachusetts
01610

High Standard Mfg. Company
1817 Dixwell Avenue
Hamden, Connecticut 06514

Intercontinental Arms, Inc.
2222 Barry Avenue
Los Angeles, California 90064

Ithaca Gun Company
Ithaca, New York 14850

Iver Johnson Arms & Cycle Works
Fitchburg, Massachusetts 01420

Marlin Firearms Co.
100 Kenna Drive
New Haven, Connecticut 06473

O. F. Mossberg & Sons, Inc.
7 Grasso Street
New Haven, Connecticut 06473

Navy Arms Company
689 Bergen Blvd.
Ridgefield, New Jersey 07657

Noble Mfg. Co., Inc.
South Main Street
Haydenville, Massachusetts 01039

Numrich Arms Corp.
West Hurley, New York 12491

Potomac Arms Corp.
P.O. Box 35-T
Alexandria, Virginia 22313

Remington Arms Company
Bridgeport, Connecticut 06602

Savage Arms Corp.
Westfield, Massachusetts 01085

Sears, Roebuck & Co.
825 South St. Louis
Chicago, Illinois 60607

Smith & Wesson, Inc.
Springfield, Massachusetts 01101

Sturm, Ruger & Co.
Southport, Connecticut 06490

Wards
619 West Chicago
Chicago, Illinois 60607

Weatherby's
2781 East Firestone Blvd.
South Gate, California 90280

Winchester Repeating Arms Co.
New Haven, Connecticut 06504

GUNS AND GUN PARTS, REPLICA AND ANTIQUE

Antique Gun Parts, Inc.
569 South Braddock Avenue
Pittsburgh, Pennsylvania 15221

Francis Bannerman's Sons, Inc.
Box 126
Blue Point, Long Island, New York 11715

Shelley Braverman
Athens, New York 12015

Dixie Gun Works, Inc.
Highway 51 South
Union City, Tennessee 38261

Ellwood Epps Sporting Goods
80 King Street
Clinton, Ontario, Canada

Numrich Arms Company
West Hurley, New York 12491

GUNS (FOREIGN)

Abercrombie & Fitch
Madison at 45th Street
New York, New York 10017

American Import Company
1167 Mission Street
San Francisco, California 94103

Browning Arms Company
Route 4, Box 624-B
Arnold, Missouri 63010

Centennial Arms Corp.
3318 West Devon
Chicago, Illinois 60645

Century Arms Company
3-5 Federal Street
St. Albans, Vermont 05478

Continental Arms Corp.
697 Fifth Avenue
New York, New York 10022

W. H. Craig
Box 927
Selma, Alabama 36701

Charles Daly, Inc.
90 Chambers Street
New York, New York 10007

Dave's House of Guns
9130 Viscount Row
Dallas, Texas 75247

Dixie Gun Works, Inc.
Highway 51 South
Union City, Tennessee 38261

Flaig's Lodge
Millvale, Pennsylvania 15209

J. L. Galef & Sons, Inc.
85 Chambers
New York, New York 10007

Garcia Sporting Arms Corp.
329 Alfred Avenue
Teaneck, New Jersey 07666

Harrington & Richardson Arms Co.
320 Park Avenue
Worcester, Massachusetts 01610

Herter's
Waseca, Minnesota 56093

Interarms Ltd.
10 Prince Street
Alexandria, Virginia 22313

International Firearms Co., Ltd.
Montreal, Quebec, Canada

Ithaca Gun Company
Terrace Hill
Ithaca, New York 14850

Paul Jaeger, Inc.
211 Leedom Street
Jenkintown, Pennsylvania 19046

Navy Arms Company
689 Bergen Blvd.
Ridgefield, New Jersey 07657

Pachmayr Gun Works
1220 S. Grand Avenue
Los Angeles, California 90015

Pacific International Import Co.
2416 16th Street
Sacramento, California 91605

Richland Arms Company
321 West Adrian Street
Blissfield, Michigan 49228

Savage Arms Corp.
Westfield, Massachusetts 01085

Stoeger Arms Company
55 Ruta Court
South Hackensack, New Jersey 07606

Tradewinds, Inc.
P.O. Box 1191
Tacoma, Washington 98401

Weatherby's
2781 Firestone Blvd.
South Gate, California 90280

GUNSMITH SUPPLIES, TOOLS, SERVICES

Alamo Heat Treating Company
Box 55345
Houston, Texas 77055

American Edestaal, Inc.
1 Atwood Avenue
Tenafly, New Jersey 07670

B-Square Company
Box 11281
Ft. Worth, Texas 76110

Brown & Sharpe Mfg. Company
Precision Park
North Kingston, Rhode Island, 02852

Bob Brownell's
Route 2
Montezuma, Iowa 50171

Maynard P. Buehler, Inc.
17 Orinda Highway
Orinda, California 94563

Christy Gun Works
875 57th Street
Sacramento, California 95819

Clymer Mfg. Company
14241 West 11 Mile Road
Oak Park, Michigan 48237

Forster Appelt Mfg. Co., Inc.
82 E. Lanark Avenue
Lanark, Illinois 61046

Gopher Shooter's Supply
Box 246
Fairbault, Minnesota 55021

H. & M.
24062 Orchard Lake Road
Farmington, Michigan 48024

Paul Jaeger, Inc.
211 Leedom Street
Jenkintown, Pennsylvania 19046

Frank Mittermeier
3577 East Tremont
New York, New York 10465

Redford Reamer Company
Box 6604
Redford Heights Station
Detroit, Michigan 48240

Richland Arms Company
321 West Adrian Street
Blissfield, Michigan 49228

Ruhr-American Corp.
South Highway No. 5
Glenwood, Minnesota 56334

L. S. Starrett Company
Athol, Massachusetts 01331

Williams Gun Sight Company
7389 Lapeer Road
Davison, Michigan 48423

SIGHTS–METALLIC, SCOPE BASES, SCOPES

B-Square Engineering Company
Box 11281
Ft. Worth, Texas 76110

Maynard P. Buehler, Inc.
17 Orinda Highway
Orinda, California 94563

Christy Gun Works
875 57th Street
Sacramento, California 95819

Conetrol Scope Mounts
Highway 123 South
Seguin, Texas 78155

Leupold
P.O. Box 688
Beaverton, Oregon 97005

Lyman Gun Sight Products
Middlefield, Connecticut
06455

Marble Arms Corp.
1120 Superior
Gladstone, Michigan 49837

Merit Gunsight Company
P.O. Box 995
Sequim, Washington 98382

Micro Sight Company
242 Harbor Blvd.
Belmont, California 94002

Poly Choke Co., Inc.
P.O. Box 296
Hartford, Connecticut 06101

Redfield Gun Sight Company
1315 South Clarkson Street
Denver, Colorado 80210

W. R. Weaver Company
Department 68
El Paso, Texas 79915

Williams Gun Sight Company
7389 Lapeer Road
Davison, Michigan 48423

Fishing

FISHING TACKLE (MANUFACTURERS, SUPPLIERS, DEALERS)

Tony Accetta & Son
932 Avenue E
Riviera Beach, Florida 33404

Acme Tackle Company
69 Bucklin Street
Providence, Rhode Island 02907

Aitken-Warner Company
427 Beech Street
Green Camp, Ohio 43322

Alladin Laboratories, Inc.
620 South 8th Street
Minneapolis, Minnesota 55404

American Sportsman Bait Company
21744 Dequindre Avenue
Warren, Michigan 48091

Angler Products, Inc.
868 Mercer Road
Butler, Pennsylvania 16001

Angler Rod Company
1426 Oakland Avenue
St. Clair, Michigan 48079

Fred Arbogast Company, Inc.
313 West North Street
Akron, Ohio 44303

Ashaway Line & Twine Manufacturing Company
Laurel Street
Ashaway, Rhode Island 02804

B & B Tackle Company
P.O. Box 220
Lufkin, Texas 75901

B & M Company
P.O. Box 231
West Point, Mississippi 39773

Jim Bagley Bait Company
P.O. Box 110
Winter Haven, Florida 33880

Bass-Buster Lures
P.O. Box 66
Amsterdam, Missouri 64723

Bay de Noc Lure Company
Box 71
Gladstone, Michigan 49837

Bead Chain Manufacturing Company
110 Mountain Grove Street
Bridgeport, Connecticut 06605

L. L. Bean, Inc.
280 Main Street
Freeport, Maine 04032

Bear Paw Tackle Company
P.O. Box 177
Farmington, Michigan 48024

Berkley & Company, Inc.
1617 Hill Avenue
Spirit Lake, Iowa 51360

Bluegill Tackle Manufacturing Company
P.O. Box 57
Fuquay Varina, North Carolina 27526

Boone Bait Company, Inc.
P.O. Box 571
Winter Park, Florida 32789

Browning Arms Company
Route 1
Morgan, Utah 84050

Brunswick Corp., Sports Div.
69 West Washington Street
Chicago, Illinois 60602

California Tackle Company, Inc.
4060 East Gage Avenue
Bell, California 90201

Cordell Tackle, Inc.
P.O. Box 2020
Hot Springs, Arkansas 71901

Cortland Line Company
67 E. Court Street
Cortland, New York 13045

Creek Club Bait Company
Garrett, Indiana 46738

Daisy Heddon Div., Victor Comptometer Corp.
414 West Street
Dowagiac, Michigan 49047

Daiwa
14011 South Normandie Avenue
Gardena, California 90249

DeLong Lures, Inc.
80 Compark Road
Centerville, Ohio 45459

Depew Manufacturing Company
359 Duffy Avenue
Hicksville, Long Island, New York 11802

DeWitt Plastics
26 Aurelius Avenue
Auburn, New York 13021

E. I. du Pont de Nemours & Co., Inc.
1007 Market Street
Wilmington, Delaware 19898

Dynaflex Manufacturing Co.
1075 West 21st Place
Hialeah, Florida 33010

F. B. Spinning Reels, Div.
Feurer Bros.
77 Lafayette Avenue
North White Plains, New York 10603

Famous Keystone Corp.
1344 West 37th Street
Chicago, Illinois 60609

The Garcia Company
329 Alfred Avenue
Teaneck, New Jersey 07666

Gladding Corporation
South Otselic, New York 13155

Gladding Corp.–South Bend Tackle Co., Inc.
4275 N.W. 77th Avenue
Miami, Florida 33148

The Gliebe Company
1154 Myrtle Avenue
Brooklyn, New York 11221

Great Lakes Products, Inc.
312 Huron Blvd.
Marysville, Michigan 48040

Harrison-Hoge Industries, Inc.
104 Arlington Avenue
St. James, New York 11780

Helin Tackle Company
4057 Beaufait
Detroit, Michigan 48207

Herter's Inc.
Waseca, Minnesota 56093

Indian Head Sporting Goods, Inc.
Ripley, Mississippi 38663

Louis Johnson Company
154 Deerfield Road
Highland Park, Illinois 60035

Johnson Outboards
Div. Outboard Marine Corp.
Sea-Horse Drive
Waukegan, Illinois 60085

Johnson Reels, Inc.
1231 Rhine Street
Mankato, Minnesota 56001

Kodiak Corporation
Van Buskin Road and Erwin
Box 467
Ironwood, Michigan 49938

Lazy Ike Corporation
512 Central Avenue
Fort Dodge, Iowa 50501

Homer LeBlanc, Inc.
Northport, Michigan 49670

H. L. Leonard Rod Company
P.O. Box 393
Central Valley, New York 10917

Martin Reel Company, Inc.
P.O. Drawer 8
Mohawk, New York 13407

Mason Tackle Company
Otisville, Michigan 48463

The Orvis Company
Union Street
Manchester, Vermont 05254

Penn Fishing Tackle Manufacturing Company
3028 West Hunting Park Ave.
Philadelphia, Pennsylvania 19132

Phillips Fly & Tackle Company
P.O. Box 188
Alexandria, Pennsylvania 16611

Phillipson Rod Company
2705 High Street
Denver, Colorado 80205

Play-mor Products, Inc.
P.O. Drawer 740
1507 Independence Avenue
Cape Girardeau, Missouri 63701

St. Croix Corporation
North Highway 13
Park Falls, Wisconsin 54552

Scientific Anglers, Inc.
4100 James Savage Road
Midland, Michigan 48640

Sevenstrand Tackle Manufacturing Company
14789 Chestnut Street
Westminster, California 92683

Shakespeare Company
241 East Kalamazoo Avenue
Kalamazoo, Michigan 49001

Storm Manufacturing Company
P.O. Box 265
Norman, Oklahoma 73069

Sunset Line & Twine Company
Jefferson and Edwin Streets
Box 691
Petaluma, California 94952

Tensor Corporation
333 Stanley Avenue
Brooklyn, New York 11207

True Temper Corporation
American Tackle Div.
1623 Euclid Avenue
Cleveland, Ohio 44115

Tycoon Fin-Nor Corporation
29 Essex Street
Maywood, New Jersey 07607

U.S. Line Company
22 Main Street
Westfield, Massachusetts 01085

Waterford Tackle Company
55 East Pike Street
Pontiac, Michigan 48058

Weber Tackle Company
133 West Ellis Street
Stevens Point, Wisconsin
54481

Woodstream Corporation
P.O. Box 327
Lititz, Pennsylvania 17543

Wright & McGill Company
1400 Yosemite Street
Denver, Colorado 80220

Zebco Div.—Brunswick Corp.
6101 East Apache Street
P.O. Box 270
Tulsa, Oklahoma 74115

INDEX

Numbers refer to item numbers, not to page numbers. Entries are included for authors, joint authors, illustrators, and editors. Major divisions are shown, followed by the subdivisions and the entry numbers of materials falling in the smaller category.

DATE DUE

			PRINTED IN U.S.A